SEED OF SATAN
ANTICHRIST

KENNETH MCRAE

ISBN:
978-0-473-56746-0 (Paperback).
978-0-473-56747-7 (Hardcover).
978-0-473-56748-4 (EPUB).
978-0-473-56749-1 (Kindle).

This work was published by Behold Messiah in Invercargill, New Zealand during 2021. All of our books and articles can be found at beholdmessiah.com.

Corrections, suggestions and all other feedback or criticism are greatly welcomed, and future revisions will take them into account. We can be contacted at beholdmessiah@gmail.com.

Behold Messiah has no responsibility for the persistence or accuracy of URLs for external or third-party internet websites referred to in this publication and does not guarantee that any content on such websites is, or will remain, accurate or appropriate.

The Chicago Manual of Style 17th Edition has been followed for the footnotes and references.

Book edited and designed by Jordan McRae.

Contents

Abbreviations

Old Testament

Gen. Genesis | Exod. Exodus | Lev. Leviticus | Num. Numbers | Deut. Deuteronomy | Josh. Joshua | Judg. Judges | Ruth | 1-2 Sam. 1-2 Samuel | 1-2 Kgs. 1-2 Kings | 1-2 Chr. 1-2 Chronicles | Ezra | Neh. Nehemiah | Esth. Esther | Job | Psa. Psalm | Prov. Proverbs | Eccl. Ecclesiastes | Song. Song of Songs | Isa. Isaiah | Jer. Jeremiah | Lam. Lamentations | Ezek. Ezekiel | Dan. Daniel | Hos. Hosea | Joel | Amos | Obad. Obadiah | Jonah | Mic. Micah | Nah. Nahum | Hab. Habakkuk | Zeph. Zephaniah | Hag. Haggai | Zech. Zechariah | Mal. Malachi.

New Testament

Matt. Matthew | Mark | Luke | John | Acts | Rom. Romans | 1-2 Cor. Corinthians | Gal. Galatians | Eph. Ephesians | Phil. Philippians | Col. Colossians | 1-2 Thess. 1-2 Thessalonians | 1-2 Tim. 1-2 Timothy | Titus | Phlm. Philemon | Heb. Hebrews | James | 1-2 Pet. 1-2 Peter | 1-2-3 John | Jude | Rev. Revelation.

Extra-Biblical

Jash. Jasher | Jub. Jubilees | Eno. Enoch. | Mac. Maccabees.

Bible Translations

KJV King James Version | NASB New American Standard Bible | NIV New International Version | NKJV New King James Version.

References

Gen. 1-2 chapters 1 to 2 | Gen. 1:2 ch. 1, verse 2 | v./vv. verse/verses | OT Old Testament | NT New Testament | Comma for chapter verses, semi-colon for different chapter or book (GEN. 1:20-22, 27-31; 3:1; COL. 2:11-12).

Preface

The legend of the Antichrist has intrigued people for almost two millennia. In the great expanse of time, many candidates have been put forward for the distinction of being this infamous character. Throughout this time there have been many who viewed him not as an enemy to be feared, but as a liberator to be welcomed. To them, he is the human personification of his father Lucifer, the bringer of light, or enlightenment.

The Bible informs us that his ascent into humanity came from within the garden of Eden. We learn how the God of creation cursed the serpent (Lucifer) for his deception perpetrated against Eve, and then the federal head of humanity, Adam. Through this act of deception, man was inducted into the life source of the tree of the knowledge of good and evil and separated from God, the source of the tree of life. God responded by imposing a curse on the serpent which established everlasting enmity between the serpent (Lucifer) and the woman (Eve), and between their respective seed or offspring (Lucifer is spiritual, Eve is biological).

> *And I will put enmity between you and the woman, and between your offspring and hers; he will crush your head, and you will strike his heel" (Gen. 3:15 NIV).*

This first prophecy in the Bible hints at two descendants from the two opposing lines, described in the New Testament simply as Christ (Messiah) and Antichrist (Anti Messiah). They are both destined to become the two human leaders who battle for supremacy over the earth and the devotion of its inhabitants.

As a Christian I obviously believe Jesus of Nazareth is to be identified as the seed of the woman. It would be his task and right to crush the serpent's head and overturn the curse imposed on

Adam and Eve and their seed or offspring for entering covenant rebellion with the serpent (GEN. 3).

But who is the ultimate seed of the serpent? The purpose of this book will be to follow the serpent line from Eden throughout history to try and identify this man. Scripture itself gives us the right to yield ourselves to this task as indicated by two significant passages in the book of Revelation regarding the Beast, the Antichrist:

> *And that no man might buy or sell, save he that had the mark, or the name of the beast, or the number of his name.* **Here is wisdom. Let him that hath understanding count the number of the beast**: *for it is the number of a man; and his number is Six hundred threescore and six (Rev. 13:17-18 KJV).*

> **"This calls for a mind with wisdom.** *The seven heads are seven hills on which the woman sits. They are also seven kings: Five have fallen, one is, the other has not yet come; but when he does come; he must remain for only a little while. The beast who once was, and now is not. is an eighth king. He belongs to the seven and is going to his destruction (Rev. 17:9-11 NIV).*

We are instructed to exercise a mind of wisdom, to think and ponder over who these seven kings are from whom this ultimate counterfeit Messiah, the eighth king, shall come. Many would consider this a needless task, but to God, whose hand is behind the holy scriptures, it seems to be the opposite. Therefore, I gave myself to study, ponder and think as clearly as possible regarding this challenge, in order that God in His goodness might grant me the necessary wisdom required to meet this challenge. My son Jordan, with no prior biblical knowledge of the task at hand, joined me in this challenge, offering his excellent research, editing, and writing skills. His many, many questions yielded significant results. I owe a huge debt of gratitude to him for his help.

For the opportunity to put this down on paper, which is not my natural talent by any means, I must thank two encouraging women. First, my schoolteacher at Nightcaps Primary School in New Zealand who taught me from ages nine to ten, Patricia McCullum. She recognised something within me worth encouraging and gave me the confidence to draw that out from within. Second, my dear sister in the faith at St. Stephens Church, Invercargill, Evelyn Gilligan, who after reading a short two-part summary of a couple sermons I shared, encouraged me to believe that I was to turn that into a book. Upon reflecting on her words, I decided to make good on her faith and Patricia McCullum's hard work fifty years earlier. Thanks are due to my good friend Mike Ladbrook who was another important link. After reading the initial draft which I can be honest in saying that it was quite poor, he nevertheless encouraged me to try and complete the book and get it published. I could not forget to thank my wife Jan for her patience over the last eighteen months as I have worked away at these two books. You cannot write a book like this without relying on the research of others who have tread this path before you. A huge debt of gratitude goes to all the authors and bible teachers for all their hard work and insight, and I have endeavoured to correctly reference their work as accurately as possible. Finally, and most importantly, I thank Jesus of Nazareth for not passing me by but having the audacity to reveal himself to me as a living reality on the 20th of November in 1989. May this volume be a blessing to him and to you, my reader.

Kenny McRae, January 2021

Introduction

At the beginning of Genesis, we are told the story of the creation of the heavens and earth, of all life, including the pinnacle of life—man himself, and his fall from divine favour. In the garden of Eden, the subjects were given access to two trees: the tree of life, which related to their union with God; and the tree of the knowledge of good and evil. To eat from the latter tree was to incur the curse of death (GEN. 2:9-17). This forbidden tree was the one point of attack for the anointed archangel Lucifer in his rebellion against God.

Even in the most perfect of circumstances, Lucifer desired to lift his heart up in pride and rebel against God. In his lust for exaltation by his own means, he craved to "be like the Most High" and take dominion over all creation for himself (ISA. 14:12; EZEK. 28:12-19). To further his own selfish purposes, he disrupted the perfect and harmonious order of the heavenly realm by convincing a third of the angelic hosts to follow in his lawless ways (REV. 12:1-4, 7-9).

The question then is the following: what caused Lucifer to look not at God, but within himself for exaltation, and to rebel against Him, from whom all things were perfect? Was he simply dissatisfied with his place in the heavenly order? Perhaps this came into question after God created man and entered a special and direct relationship with them. In the pride of his own heart, Lucifer may have felt his place of honour, authority, and communion with God had been stolen by the inferior man (GEN. 1:28; 2:7). Out of jealousy, or perhaps seeing an opportunity to usurp God's rule, might he have strived henceforth to take authority over man in place of God by implicating them in his rebellion?

Lucifer would have been emboldened by his successful rebellion in the heavenly realm. Surely to achieve the same in the earthly realm would seem to him to be trivial in contrast.[1]

In response to the angelic rebellion, God set aside a place totally separate from Him and all His goodness, known to us as Hell. The angelic rebels are to be cast into Hell after—and only after—a final judgement by God is rendered that is fully righteous and beyond reproach (MATT. 25:41). After this time, the reality of His greatness above all others will be unequivocally accepted by all and balance will be restored. God needs not to prove this to Himself—but by doing so, avoids a situation of loyalty to Him predicated on fear rather than true reverence. In a once and for all act, God will righteously judge His enemies yet win the hearts of all who choose to be faithful. Love and truth united in justice are to be the motivating factors for loyalty. Judgement in wrath by God is his final act after every other means has been exhausted (HAB. 3:2; EXOD. 34:6-7; JAMES 2:12-13; MATT. 5:7).

The Great Deception

"You will not certainly die," the serpent (Lucifer) reassured the woman, "for God knows that when you eat from it your eyes will be opened, and you will be like God, knowing good and evil" (GEN. 3:4-5). The serpent planted the perception that God was withholding the means of *true* exaltation from Adam and Eve, while he was there to illuminate them. In truth, man was given the same freedom of choice offered to the angels, even after God suffered from their betrayal. To trust in the perfect judgement of God and follow His instructions, or follow the ways of the serpent.

---

[1] There are indications of this being the timeline of events, but ultimately this is unknown to man. Remember when God challenged Job by asking him "where were you when I laid the earth's foundation? ... while the morning stars sang together and all the angels shouted for joy? (JOB 38:4-7). God revealed that all the angels participated in the celebration of His new creation, suggesting that this was pre-rebellion. But all could still refer solely to all the faithful angels. Another possibility is that the angelic realm rebelled after Lucifer had successfully deceived Adam and Eve, realising a truly unique opportunity to challenge the legitimacy of God had been presented.

In tempting man away from faithfulness to their creator, the serpent opened the possibility of man reaching out for another pathway to exaltation—to become gods on their own terms. At least that is how it is presented. Consider how this promise was given by the most cunning and adept deceiver of all. What could be the ulterior motives? Lucifer had already challenged the supremacy of God and taken a third of the angels into his rebellion (Rev. 12:4). Why should we assume man would be left to their own devices?

> *When the woman saw that the fruit of the tree was good for food and pleasing to the eye, and desirable for gaining wisdom, she took some and ate it. She also gave some to her husband, who was with her, and he ate it. Then the eyes of both were opened, and they realized they were naked; so, they sewed fig leaves together and made coverings for themselves (Gen. 6:7 NIV).*

And here the sin nature was inherited. Sin as transgression, lawlessness, and rebellion. Our humanity became embedded with the *body of sin,* and consequently, a *body of death,* which doomed us to an inescapable end (Rom. 6:6; 7:24). The same self-seeking desire that led to rebellion and chaos in the heavenly realm was introduced into the earthly realm. Man discarded the "thou shall not" (Gen. 2:17) ordered by God in favour of the promise by the serpent to "be as gods" (Gen. 3:5).

To ourselves we were gods, insofar as we related good and evil on our terms. Even still, God would not abandon us, and pleaded with us to look upon Him for guidance. Until the time of reconciliation, God would give man every opportunity to be free, even if that freedom ultimately separated man from Himself and united man with His enemy.

Repentance—that is the ability to think again and humble oneself and turn back to God for forgiveness and reconciliation—must also be of man's own volition. It cannot be forced or simply a matter of fate—the relationship must be genuine. Man cannot be excused from the consequences of his actions and can only be forgiven from a basis of righteousness if God is to remain just, and therefore good. If the rebel angels are to be righteously judged for the exact same transgression, it would be contradictory of a just and immutable God to make an arbitrary exception for man. To deny His own nature would void any fair and legitimate judgement He could possibly cast upon Lucifer and his angels (2 TIM. 2:12-13; HEB. 6:13-18). God must therefore balance mercy with justice.

I personally think God *did* extend the same mercy to Lucifer by offering a final chance of repentance in the tree of the knowledge of good and evil. Lucifer's fate was placed entirely in his own hands, and yet he acted upon the inclinations of his rebellious heart by tempting Eve away from God and into his rebellion. The chance for redemption here through humble submission to God was the other, more sensible option (LUKE 15:11-32). Nevertheless, he willfully chose the former, and for that there is now no going back for him or the Most High. Enmity will always and forever be the disposition between them (GEN. 3:15).

The Redemptive Protoevangelium

Immediately after the fall of man into Lucifer's rebellion, the merciful and loving God declared a prophetic plan for man's redemption—the protoevangelium, or first messianic gospel of salvation:

> The woman said, "The serpent deceived me, and I ate." So, the Lord God said to the serpent: "Because you have done this ... I will put enmity between you and the woman, and between your seed and her Seed; He shall bruise your head, and you shall bruise His heel" (Gen. 3:13-15 NKJV).

We are told from the beginning of mankind that a man is destined to come from the seed or offspring of the woman (Eve) to challenge the seed of the accursed serpent (Lucifer). The seed of the woman is biological (human Eve), but the seed of the serpent is spiritual (spirit Lucifer). The seed of the woman is favoured by God—it is the godly line by birth—but the seed of the serpent is cursed by God—it is the ungodly line by spiritual alignment.[2]

The man to come from the seed of the woman challenges the serpent by suffering on our behalf as the Messiah. His heel is bruised but the serpent's head is crushed. While this will not be explored in this book, as a Christian I believe this man could only be Jesus, the one both divine and man, who, being uniquely absent of sin was not cursed under the covenant. He descended from his heavenly place with the Father and sacrificed himself *for* man, *as* a man, so we may be restored into God's presence. He voluntarily subjected himself to the covenant man cut with the serpent and redeemed mankind from within. This was necessary because to cut a new covenant with man, God first had to break the Luciferic covenant so the curse of sin therein could be nullified. The curse of sin which necessitated our death was defeated after his death and resurrection—it died with him but did not rise with him (GAL. 3:13-14; DEUT. 21:23). Having defeated sin and death, the Abrahamic promise for all peoples of the earth to be blessed was realised. Restoration to eternal life was made available to all who die in Christ and are born again, free from the curse of death. Paul put it perfectly in Romans: "just as one trespass resulted in condemnation for all people, so also one righteous act resulted in justification and life for all people ... just as sin reigned in death, so also grace might reign through righteousness to bring eternal life through Jesus Christ our Lord" (ROM. 5:18, 21).

The Luciferic covenant had been ratified by Adam and Eve and symbolically affirmed by eating the forbidden fruit. Jesus allowed us to cut a new covenant with God ratified by faith, and

---

[2] The seed of the serpent is based on spiritual descendancy, not biological. This topic has been poisoned by a racist fringe who posit that Cain was the biological son of Lucifer and use this to denigrate those they claim are the accursed "serpent seed." This is a baseless view, for it is explicitly said that Cain was the son of Adam and Eve (GEN. 4:1). There are certainly peoples who are generally considered to be ungodly, such as the line of Cain, the Canaanites in particular, or even the sons of Esau, the brother of Jacob, the Edomites and Amalekites. However, individuals are not judged based on their blood.

symbolically affirmed by partaking in his flesh and blood through the bread and wine (JOHN 6:45-59; LUKE 22:19-20; MATT. 26:26-28; 1 COR. 10:16-17; 11:23-26).

The Binary Choice for Man

C. S. Lewis perfectly encapsulated our binary situation in his classic work *Mere Christianity*:

> *God created things with free will. That means creatures which can go either wrong or right. Some people think they can imagine a creature that was free and had no possibility of going wrong; I cannot. If a thing is free to be good it is also free to go bad. Why then did God give us free will? Because free will, though it makes evil possible, also is the only thing that makes love or goodness or joy worth having ... If God thinks this state of war in the universe a price worth paying for free will- that is for making a live world in which creatures can do real, good or harm and something of real importance can happen, instead of a toy world which only moves when he pulls the strings-then we may take it that it is worth paying.[3]*

Godly Line

Those of the godly line have one way to the God of the tree of life, and that is through faith in His Word for guidance and spiritual revelation. There is either faith or unbelief, with no third option available. True biblical faith directs our efforts away from personal god realisation towards encounter with the living God Himself. All that is asked of us is to understand and accept that it is the promised descendant of the woman who makes this restored union possible by crushing the serpent's head through an act of self-denial and sacrifice. Our exaltation is dependent entirely upon the righteous character of God, imparted to those who

---

[3] Lewis, *Mere Christianity*, 47-49.

believe in the great reconciling work of the one destined to fulfil the work of the seed of the woman. By grace (unmerited mercy) He grants the repentant spiritual revelation of this truth so they may be freed from the lie of self-Godhood told by the serpent (ROM. 3:21-31; 4:20-25; 8:14-17; EPH. 2:10).

Ungodly Line

The ungodly line glorifies the doctrine of self-Godhood preached by the serpent, directing us to be wise in our own eyes, and to claim for ourselves what we accept as right and wrong or good or evil. The road to salvation for the ungodly is entirely relative—it is purely of our own choosing. The suggested antidote to the suffering and loss of meaning we endure is in the serpent's promise to "be as gods" (GEN. 3:4-5). These sentiments are echoed in the ancient mystery religions, and in the current ecumenical movement which is pushing us towards religious homogeneity. By these means he shall prepare the world for his own seed, who shall endeavour to take the place and honour of the seed of the woman, and reign as king over all creation. As elaborated by C.S. Lewis, a civil war is playing out in the earthly affairs of men as it is in the heavenly domain.

Conclusion

In this book we will follow the bloodline of the serpent line through history to try and correctly identify its ultimate seed or offspring. In the companion book on the godly line, we shall demonstrate beyond question that Jesus of Nazareth bears all the scriptural watermarks relating to the promised seed of the woman.

1

Origins of the Ungodly Adversaries

God successfully executed His masterful counterplan to redeem fallen man and vindicate Himself before the accusatory Lucifer and the rebel angels. Jesus, the seed of the woman, was the answer from the very beginning. When he came and died on our behalf, he created a pathway of restoration for us through a New Covenant (HEB. 9:15-28). As it was before the fall, the choice between everlasting life (tree of life) or a temporary life of self-will and earthly indulgences (tree of the knowledge of good and evil) is put before us. Every one of us are free to remain under the Luciferic covenant that was ratified by Adam and Eve when they ate the forbidden fruit, or having been freed from its grip, remake a covenant with God by faith, and ratify it by partaking in the flesh and blood of Jesus to experience his death and resurrection (JOHN 6:45-59; ROM. 6:3-4).

In any scenario, Lucifer answers to God alone—the approval of man does not change his fate. All he is left with is one desperate option to evade judgement and condemnation into Hell, and that is to prove God a liar in relation to His own prophetic word. The only clear point-of-attack is to eradicate God's chosen people of Israel and the Church. Doing so would undermine God's promise that Israel would always be a people before Him, and that the gates of Hell would not prevail against His church of Christ (JER. 31:35-37; 33:25-26; MATT. 16:18). If the Word of God here can be rendered invalid, Lucifer will not only successfully defend himself from

God's judgement, but he will be justified in pulling God under *his* judgement.

Despite the precarious situation, I do not for one second believe that Lucifer is working in this final conflict from a mental position of defeat simply because scripture declares that he is a defeated foe. He believes not just that he *can* win, but that he *will* win. Satan knows that Hell is waiting for him if he comes up short in this final battle. To be stripped of all authority, distinction, honour, and power is no doubt a prospect he cannot bear the thought of (DAN. 12:2). That which he exalts in is of no meaning and is without application in that God-forsaken place.

Now that he is granted only a lowly endowment of dominion over the earth, Lucifer must work entirely through man to carry out his objectives. The ultimate goal being to manifest within the seed of the serpent, the Antichrist. Once again, two pathways to enlightenment and truth are presented to us. Two opposing seed lines from which we must choose one, willingly or not. Here lies the foundation of his desperate strategy for earth. It is now up to us to explore his outworking throughout history to try and predict that which is to come until he and the Antichrist are finally defeated.

The Ungodly Trinity

The major players from the perspective of the serpent line are the ungodly trinity of Satan or Lucifer (dragon), the Antichrist (beast) and the False Prophet (REV. 16:13; 20:2, 10). Predictably, they mimic the work of God the Father, Jesus the Son, and the Holy Spirit.

Satan or Lucifer

The chosen human vessel of Lucifer to counterfeit the true light of Jesus is hinted at within both the Old and New Testaments. The prophet Isaiah talked of the mercy God will show to Jacob and the house of Israel, and how he will set them in their own land and give them rest—an eternal rest (ISA. 14:1-32). Judging by the continuing discrimination and warfare that still afflicts them, this time of eternal rest has yet to come. God has promised that at the time this eternal rest actuates, the people of Israel will take up a proverb against the King of Babylon (Antichrist) and ask "how has the oppressor ceased" who ruled the nations in anger (Vv. 4-7). His judgement, as well as the promised rest for Israel, are concurrent events that occur after Jesus returns in glory (REV. 19:11-21; 20:1-6). Hell becomes his habitation and all there marvel at his arrival, exclaiming "so you have become as weak as we" (ISA. 14:9-10). In this same context, Isaiah identifies this figure as "Lucifer, son of the morning" (ISA. 14:12). Notice his emphasis on *I* over the next two verses:

> *"How you are fallen from heaven, O Lucifer, son of the morning! How you are cut down to the ground, you who weakened the nations! For you have said in your heart: 'I will ascend into heaven, I will exalt my throne above the stars of God; I will also sit on the mount of the congregation on the farthest sides of the north; I will ascend above the heights of the clouds, I will be like the Most High.' Yet you shall be brought down to Sheol, to the lowest depths of the Pit" (Isa. 14:12-15 NKJV).*

This was Lucifer's attitude and rebellion in the heavenly realm, a rebellion he brought into the earthly realm through his deception of God's earthly regents, Adam and Eve. He promoted the self to a place of deification, and man has taken it upon himself to promote this ideal unceasingly. He hopes to bring the rebellion of self-worship to its conclusion through his earthly seed—the Antichrist, here called the Assyrian (ISA. 10:20-34; 14:24-27).

The prophet Ezekiel revealed crucial details on the figure of Satan or Lucifer, and his earthly spawn in the Antichrist. In chapter 28 we learn of the *prince* of Tyre, and the *king* of Tyre. Theologians relate both figures to either Hiram I or Ithobaal I, but it is my personal contention that the king is the spiritual power behind the earthly prince of Tyre—the physical ruler. In this view, I consider the prince of Tyre to be the Antichrist, and the king of

Tyre his spiritual father in Satan. I will discuss the connection to the Antichrist in the following section. For now, we will read the abridged description of the king of Tyre which seems to be far more fitting of a primordial being like Satan:

> *"Son of man, take up a lamentation for the king of Tyre, and say to him, 'Thus says the Lord God: "You were the seal of perfection, full of wisdom and perfect in beauty. You were in Eden, the garden of God; Every precious stone was your covering ... "you were the anointed cherub who covers; I established you; You were on the holy mountain of God; You walked back and forth in the midst of fiery stones. You were perfect in your ways from the day you were created, till iniquity was found in you. "By the abundance of your trading you became filled with violence within, and you sinned; Therefore, I cast you as a profane thing out of the mountain of God; And I destroyed you, O covering cherub, From the midst of the fiery stones. "Your heart was lifted up because of your beauty; You corrupted your wisdom for the sake of your splendor; I cast you to the ground, I laid you before kings, that they might gaze at you. "You defiled your sanctuaries by the multitude of your iniquities, By the iniquity of your trading; Therefore I brought fire from your midst; It devoured you, And I turned you to ashes upon the earth in the sight of all who saw you. All who knew you among the peoples are astonished at you; You have become a horror, and shall be no more forever""*
> *(Ezek. 28:11-19 NKJV).*

The parallels to Lucifer here are abundantly clear, and do not seem to correspond to a mere human king. While I believe this depicts Lucifer as a spiritual king of Tyre, he too, will reign as an earthly king of Tyre through his coming seed. Isaiah and Ezekiel both qualify this statement through their testimony of a wicked *earthly* king who is the seed of a wicked *heavenly* king—Satan manifested in the flesh. Once again he seeks to mirror the seed of the woman who is God manifested in the flesh.

Numerical Signature of Lucifer

There are various names given to Lucifer which bear a numerical signature of thirteen in the original Greek of the New Testament. That is because for each letter in the Greek alphabet (and the Hebrew) there is a corresponding numeric value. This numeric dimension to the language was employed in the writing of the Old and New Testaments to provide deeper levels of meaning. The process of computing the numeric values of words or phrases is called *gematria* in Hebrew and *isopsephy* in Greek. Below is an example of this concept in action to find connections between the different names of Lucifer:

Image 1.1 – Greek isopsephy (numeric values) of Lucifer's names

NAME	VALUE	FORMULA
Dragon	975	13 x 75
Tempter	1053	13 x 81
Belial	78	13 x 6
Murderer	1820	13 x 40
Serpent	780	13 x 60
Called the Devil and Satan	2197	13 x 13 x 13
The Serpent, called the Devil and Satan	2977	13 x 229

Another example of gematria is in the Hebrew word used for serpent in the Bible, *nahash*—the same word for the serpent in the garden of Eden. The Hebrew gematria value for *nahash* is 358, the same as *Mashiach* (Messiah). The seed of the serpent is of course, a Messiah or Christ (transliterated from the Greek word for messiah, *christos*) in opposition to the true Messiah (Antichrist).

Lucifer as the Serpent

Moving on from gematria now, we will investigate the link between Lucifer and the serpent. Speaking of the restoration of Israel to come, Isaiah described the day in which the Lord will "punish Leviathan the fleeing serpent ... even Leviathan the twisted serpent; and he will kill the dragon who lives in the sea" (ISA. 27:1). Notice how he conflates the sea monster Leviathan with the serpent and the dragon. These terms all point to a singular figure, and Satan just so happens to fit these descriptors. Leviathan is described by God as a fearsome creature without equal on earth. He is subject to no one but God. Not simply a crocodile or other sea-creature, it breathes fire like a dragon (JOB 41:18-21). Considering the context of the book of Job, the connection to Satan, who is also described as a serpent and a dragon, can be fairly made. In the final verse describing Leviathan, the connection is strengthened: "He looks on everything that is high; He is king over all the sons of pride" (JOB 41:33-34). Does this not resemble the serpent who exalted himself above the Most High? Psalm 74 explicitly ties the two figures together by referencing the prophecy made to the serpent in the garden of Eden, that his head will be crushed by the Messiah (GEN. 3:15).

> *Yet God is my King from long ago, who performs acts of salvation in the midst of the earth. You divided the sea by Your strength; You broke the heads of the sea monsters in the waters. You crushed the heads of Leviathan; You gave him as food for the creatures of the wilderness (Psa. 74:12-14 NASB).*

The prophet Isaiah, when speaking of the time of everlasting salvation, attested to this reality: "was it not You [God] who cut Rahab in pieces, who pierced the dragon?" (ISA. 51:9). Job also: "With His power He quieted the sea, and by His understanding He shattered Rahab. By His breath the heavens are cleared; His hand has pierced the fleeing serpent" (JOB 26:11-13). The Hebrew word for dragon used here is *tannin*, which can refer more broadly to serpents (JOB 7:12; EXOD. 7:9-12; DEUT. 32:33; NEH. 2:13; PSA. 148:7; JER. 51:34). In this context, where Rahab is used as an emblematic name for Egypt, the dragon or serpent is most likely the crocodile, the symbol of Egypt. The Pharaoh of Egypt is often compared with the crocodile (PSA. 34:13-14; EZEK. 29:3; 32:2).

These verses paint a picture of the future judgement of Lucifer, the greater Pharaoh of a kingdom greater than Egypt, or Rahab. The biblical imagery surrounding the sea is of unregenerate humanity, the sons of pride who war against the knowledge of the true God. The Leviathan who dwells there is none other than Lucifer, whose head will finally be crushed as the final act of salvation (PSA. 74:12-14; GEN. 3:15).

Antichrist

As outlined in the introduction, the motivation behind this book is to identify the Antichrist (1 JOHN 2:18-22; 4:2-3; 2 JOHN 1:7), the seed or son of the serpent (Satan). Depending on the context, the word Antichrist can simply describe the spirit of the present evil age, or those in opposition to the true Christ, but Antichrist in the singular denotes the eschatological figure revealed by God after the fall. It is he who is soon to mount the final challenge against the Most High on earth within a global empire. All of man is fated to follow one of two Christ figures, and their eternal destiny depends on their decision. For this reason, it is imperative that we are well-educated on who these two Christs are who seek our allegiance, and the signs of their coming. Each subsequent chapter of this book will examine different aspects of the Antichrist, the man of sin and lawlessness (2 THESS. 2:3) using biblical testimony, together with supporting evidence from non-canonical, occult, rabbinical, and historical texts. We will trace his ungodly lineage, both spiritual and biological, outline the potential empire from which he will rise, and consider the attributes he will inherit from previous kings. Together, these elements will produce a composite image of the Antichrist we are to expect on the world stage and help us understand the mechanisms behind his ascension.

The Assyrian

Before we continue, remember how in the section on Satan I alluded to the Assyrian from the prophecy of Isaiah (ISA. 10:5-20-34; 14:24-27). He, I believe, is identified with the Antichrist. The Babylonians defeated the Assyrians and became the dominant power but the spirit of the Assyrian (Antichrist) persisted in the kingdom of Babylon. We heard from Isaiah how the Assyrian smote the people with a continual stroke, which is to say the evil spirit underlying the Assyrian corrupted each successive gentile kingdom. But Isaiah reassured us that there will come a time when his yoke and burden upon the people will be lifted when God destroys him in his own land. Just as judgement was executed on both the former kingdoms of Assyria and Babylon, God will judge the final embodiment of this Assyrian-Babylonian mindset, the Antichrist, and his world kingdom.

In this line of interpretation, the king of Babylon and the Assyrian are in fact one and the same—the future seed of the serpent, the Antichrist. In the day that judgement is executed on him in wrath is the same day his yoke (and his spiritual father, Satan) is forever removed from Israel and they finally enter the messianic age of eternal rest. The Apostle Paul tells us all creation is waiting for this great future event—for it will signal the resurrection from the dead:

> *We know that the whole creation has been groaning as in the pains of childbirth right up to the present time. Not only so, but we ourselves, who have the firstfruits of the Spirit, groan inwardly as we wait eagerly for our adoption to sonship, the redemption of our bodies. For in this hope, we were saved. But hope that is seen is no hope at all. Who hopes for what they already have? (Rom. 8:22-24 NIV).*

The prophet Ezekiel provided another perspective on the wicked ruler to come, the Antichrist (EZEK. 28:1-19). In the original context, Ezekiel is speaking of the prince of Tyre (Phoenicia) who I believe to be Hiram I (rabbinical sources concur) though some take it to mean Ithobaal I (Vv. 1-10). Like many biblical prophecies, I believe there to be double fulfilment here—the prince of Tyre also points to the Antichrist, the Assyrian. Ezekiel places great emphasis on the godlike wisdom of the prince, claiming him to be wiser than Daniel, who likely was the wisest natural man who has ever lived (Vv. 3-4). This man who claims divinity is told he will die like an uncircumcised man and have his brightness defiled (Vv. 28:6-10). He acts in the character of his spiritual father and claims himself to be the light—just as Lucifer does as light bearer. His claims to Godhood are out of arrogance, not based in truth, and the true God will reveal it.

Coming Manifestation of the Antichrist and His Judgement

As we revealed in the previous section, the king of Tyre whom Ezekiel discussed in the chapter is Satan, the spiritual power behind the prince of Tyre, the Antichrist. Ezekiel finished the chapter with a proclamation of judgement on Sidon or Zidon, the sister city of Tyre in Phoenicia. It will be destroyed after the Lord restores Israel and is sanctified in them before the nations (Vv. 20-26). While the Hebrews under Jacob stayed in Egypt to survive the great famine throughout the lands, the Canaanites under Sidon, the grandson of Ham, established a foothold in their land to ensure the descendants of Abraham did not return. Their settlement here allowed for the rise of the Phoenician gods and their mighty rebellion. It was a perfect place from which the promised seed of the serpent could ascend. It is here that his power base in the earth is centred and has grown outward to all peoples through the agency of the ancient mystery religions.

In the meantime, God has restrained these evil forces. First it was to protect the lineage of the promised godly seed in Jesus, and after his death, it was to provide a large window of time for the Church to grow its harvest. But God declares that a day is coming when that hand of restraint will be removed for a time and all the forces of evil will be granted the opportunity to be fully expressed

(2 Thess. 2:5-10). These forces of evil will converge to produce its fullest manifestation in the personage of the Antichrist, the man of sin (2 Thess. 3-4). He will exalt himself above all other gods and blaspheme the Most High God (Dan. 7:25; 11:36-39; 2 Thess. 2:3-4). To assist in his ascendancy to god status on earth, Satan endows him with all the supernatural powers and wonders for deception. The ultimate deceptive work will be to resurrect from the dead after receiving a deadly head wound (2 Thess. 2:9; Rev. 13:3-8). The people of the world who were unconvinced by the resurrection of Christ will worship the Antichrist *as* Christ, and seat him as God in the Third Temple (2 Thess. 2:3-4; Rev. 13:3-8). From his seat in the Temple of God he will *demand* the worship of mankind by requiring them to receive his mark as a symbol of their loyalty (Rev. 13:16-18; 14:9-11; 15:2; 16:2; 19:20; 20:4). This time of tribulation under the Antichrist will be given unto his hand for three-and-a-half years (Dan. 7:25; Rev. 13:3-6).

False Prophet

In the same way the Holy Spirit honours and empowers the son, the False Prophet does unto the beast. With this assistance, the beast will rapidly ascend to fame, power, and ultimately, absolute authority. The description of the False Prophet as looking like a lamb, but speaking like a dragon, indicates he will be a smooth and convincing promoter, but will be wearing a mask to hide the reality of his nature (Rev. 13:11).

He will act in the role of Elijah the prophet who was promised to come before the great and dreadful day of the Lord (Mal. 4:5-6). He will duplicate Elijah's miracle of calling down fire from heaven to the astonishment of the world and prime them for the revelation of the Beast (1 Kgs. 18:38; Rev. 13:13-14). He will also act in the character of Moses by administering the false covenant for the people to follow (Rev. 13:11-17) in opposition to the God-given covenants (Deut. 6:8). Consider how it was Moses and Elijah who appeared atop Mount Hermon, the domain of their ungodly adversaries, with Jesus and the disciples (Matt. 17:1–8; Mark 9:2–8;

LUKE 9:28–36). This was a picture of the end days battle when the two witnesses (Moses and Elijah) return to prepare the way for Jesus again (REV. 11). The significance of Mount Hermon as a demonic centre of great importance will be explored in the following chapter.

The forerunner of Elijah during the first coming of Jesus was John the Baptist, and he prepared the way for Jesus as Messiah (MATT. 3:1-12). Moses himself warned the Israelites that they must listen to the prophet God was going to send after him, that being Jesus Christ (DEUT. 18:15—19). Just as Moses and Elijah were the advocates and voices which lead the way for the true Messiah, the False Prophet will be the same for the false Messiah to come, the Antichrist (EXOD. 20:18-20; 1 KGS. 5:17-18; 18:38; 2 KGS. 1:10).

Conclusion

Lucifer the light-bearer has successfully brought his counterfeit light from the heavenly domain into the earth through the deception at Eden. Consequently, man has come to embrace this counterfeit light and take on the inward disposition of sin. Most people have no idea that they are presently in the counterfeit light and are being drawn ever further into it, while being made ever more distant from the true light centred in the God of creation. Throughout the rest of this book, we will share this ongoing process and the major players involved in preparation for the arrival of the ultimate man of light, the seed of the serpent.

2

The Serpent Line on Earth

The book of Genesis provides paired genealogies of two lines of antediluvians ... the line of Cain can be designated as the "secular" line, for the sole achievements of the different generations seem to be related to their material accomplishments. The line of Seth introduces a religious, if not moral, distinction between the two lines, by mentioning the righteousness of Enoch, followed by Noah and the flood narrative – William H. Shea.[4]

I n a similar fashion to our examination of the godly line in the companion book "Seed of God: Jesus Christ," we shall examine the notable men who answered the calling of the serpent from the corresponding ungodly line. Together they work to provide a composite image of the serpent seed to come, the Antichrist. As a purely spiritual lineage, each of these men relate back to the serpent in character and in continual defiance of God. God would allow them back into His house if through repentance and sincere faith they accepted Him back into their hardened hearts—but this very attitude is their defining characteristic. The inward disposition of the ungodly is an inward dissatisfaction with God's rule and oversight, and a desire to supersede Him through

---

[4] Shea, "The Antediluvians."

their own perceived natural talents and strength. Truth acquired through natural, material, or occult means is always given precedence over the Word of God.

Freemason Rudolf Steiner perfectly summarised the enmity that exists between the two seeds and the clear differences in their attitudes and goals from the perspective of the ungodly line:

> *The whole conception underlying the creation story according to the Temple Legend is based upon the fact that there is a kind of enmity between Jehovah and everything which is derived from the other Elohim [Lucifer] and their descendants, the 'Sons of Fire' — this being the designation of the descendants of Cain according to the Temple Legend. Jehovah creates enmity between Cain and his race, and Abel and his race ... The arch-enmity which exists between those who receive their existence from the divine worlds, and those who work out everything for themselves.*[5]

Beginnings at Cain

From the very first generation after the fall of humanity, the two seed lines became manifested on earth. The firstborn son of man was Cain, the first son of Adam. In contrast to his godly brother Abel, Cain was the first of fallen man to exhibit the new reality of sin, encapsulated by his murder of Abel. The descendants of Cain would come to characterise the nature of the serpent (ungodly) line, becoming more entrenched in sin and wickedness after each passing generation. We shall follow the notable figures in the line of Cain until its biological termination via the great flood. Because the same spiritual force that inhabited them is what each subsequent generation contends with, their stories and character still serve to illustrate the man of sin to come (2 THESS. 2:3).

---

[5] Steiner, *The Temple Legend,* lecture 7.

Cain

Eve gave birth to Cain after God expelled her from the garden of Eden to a life of toil, hardship, and uncertainty. In her delight she cried out "I have acquired a man from the Lord," expressing her hope that this child would be the one to crush the serpent's head and sever man's union with the serpent which she had brought upon mankind (GEN. 4:1). She then conceived again and gave birth to another son called Abel (V. 4:2).

Both Cain and Abel seemed to have understood the need for sacrifice, probably being aware of how the animal skin God procured for their parents was also a spiritual covering, a substitutionary atonement. Like their parents, they found themselves needing their own covering, as they were the first humans to be *born* with a sin nature. In the course of time Cain brought some of the fruits of the soil as an offering to the Lord. The second born Abel also brought an offering—fat portions from the best of his flock, the firstfruits (VV. 4:3-4). God respected Abel and his offering but did not respect Cain and his offering (VV. 4:4-5). This passage perfectly illustrates the difference between the godly and ungodly lines, and what is and is not pleasing to God.

Cain offered the works of his own hands—the crops from the land—as if it were God and not himself who lacked. It was simply a sacrifice of acknowledgement. He did not respect the need for atonement for sin, believing himself righteous in his own eyes. Abel on the other hand, came to God acutely aware of his sinfulness and recognised atonement could not come from works, but from God. The substitutionary atonement of the best of his flock was a testament to his faith in the promised great sacrifice. That being the substitutionary sacrifice of Jesus, the firstfruits of the dead. Abel understood that such a mediator of God (Jesus) was required to be purified and justified in the ways of God (GEN. 4:4; HEB. 9:14, 27-28; 10:12-17).

The Freemason Rudolf Steiner echoed the crucial distinction between the two sons, even if he was more sympathetic to the individualism of Cain:

> *The fact that Abel makes the sacrifice of an animal to Jehovah, while Cain brings the fruits of the earth, is an illustration ... of this contrast between the race of Cain and the race of Abel. Cain has to wrest from the earth with hard labour the fruits which are necessary for the sustenance of mankind; Abel takes what is already living, what has been prepared for his livelihood. The race of Cain creates, as it were, the living out of the lifeless. Abel takes up what is already alive, what is already imbued with the breath of life. Abel's sacrifice is pleasing to God, but Cain's is not.[6]*

Because Cain rejected the authority of God and trusted the works of his own hands over God, naturally the most base and barbaric human inclinations swelled up within him. Jealousy of his brother filled his heart. God challenged his attitude, encouraging Cain to take control over the sin that desired to master him, but he wilfully rejected that advice and jealousy escalated to murder (GEN. 4:3-8). When God asked Cain where his brother Abel was, Cain contemptuously replied, "I don't know. Am I my brother's keeper?" (V. 4:9). He had no fear of God. Such a lack of respect towards God is the defining characteristic of unrepentant man.

In an act of grace, God placed a mark upon Cain, so, if anyone killed Cain, vengeance would be exacted seven times upon that person (VV. 4:13-15). Here we would expect Abel to receive his due justice, but instead God pronounced a strange curse—not upon Cain, but upon any potential killer of Cain. I believe we can make sense of this dilemma once we continue along the ungodly line.

It is said that following this, "Cain went out from the Lord's presence and lived in the land of Nod [meaning exile], east of Eden" where he established the first city, Enoch (VV. 4:16-17). Because Cain ventured out from the presence of God in the east, this cardinal direction thus became associated with the light of the ancient mysteries. It symbolised the separation from God into the

---

[6] Ibid.

wilderness of self-will and self-preservation. The north on the other hand, is associated with the location of God's presence (Isa. 14:13-14). Occult practitioners deem the north to be the place of darkness, and the east to be the true light.

The first-century historian and Jewish aristocrat Flavius Josephus stated in *Antiquities of the Jews* how Cain was not accepting of his punishment once in the land of Nod, but chose instead to increase his wickedness:

> *He augmented his household substance with much wealth, by rapine and violence; he excited his acquaintance to procure pleasures and spoils by robbery, and became a great leader of men into wicked courses. He also introduced a change in that way of simplicity wherein men lived before; and was the author of measures and weights. And whereas they lived innocently and generously while they knew nothing of such arts, he changed the world into cunning craftiness.*[7]

Due to his hardened ways of wickedness, "even while Adam was alive, it came to pass that the posterity of Cain became exceedingly wicked, every one … more wicked than the former."[8] Now we shall look to illustrate how his progeny, and those aligned with them, inherited his wickedness and ungodliness.

Lamech

The symbolism of the sevenfold vengeance which God promised on behalf of Cain is attached to his sixth-generation descendant Lamech (Gen. 4:13-19). The biblical account of Lamech includes an admission of murder which resembles that of his murderous ancestor, Cain. In a scene of lamentation to his wives, Lamech told them that he had killed a young man for hurting him, and that "if Cain shall be avenged seven times, then Lamech seventy-seven

---

[7] Josephus, "Antiquities of the Jews," 1.60.
[8] Ibid.

times!" (GEN. 4:23-24). Lois Tverberg observed that Lamech not only inherited Cain's lust for violence and revenge, but he was willing to "outdo God in revenge ... not just sevenfold, but seventy-sevenfold."[9]

The non-canonical, but frequently biblically referenced book of Jasher (JOSH. 10:13; 2 SAM. 1:18; 2 TIM. 3:8) offers insight into the meaning of this passage. We are told a story of how Lamech accidentally killed Cain after confusing him for an animal in the field (JASH. 2:26-29). Lamech was at this time advanced in his years and could hardly see, and his son Tubal-Cain who was with him told Lamech "to draw his bow" and shoot Cain who was far in the distance. According to Jasher, this was judgement from God for the "wickedness which he had done to his brother Abel, according to the word of the Lord which he had spoken." What was the word he had spoken to Cain? It was the promise to enact vengeance on whoever kills him seven times over (GEN. 4:13-15). Tubal-Cain was the one responsible for his death, and he was the seventh-generation descendant of Cain. The mark which God placed on Cain was a grace-period lasting seven generations until Tubal-Cain. If repentance were shown, judgement would be averted, and if anyone frustrated its fulfilment by killing Cain, the seven-times judgement would fall on them. The interplay between judgement and mercy here is reinforced in the New Testament when Jesus directly referenced the seven symbolism of Cain and Lamech:

> *Then Peter came up and said to Him, "Lord, how many times shall my brother sin against me and I still forgive him? Up to seven times?" Jesus said to him, "I do not say to you, up to seven times, but up to seventy-seven times. (Matt. 18:21-22 NASB).*

Tverberg aptly observed how Jesus flipped the message of vengeance into forgiveness, showing how God (Jesus) always adds provisions for mercy within his warnings of judgement:

---

[9] Tverberg, "Lamech's Opposite."

Jesus may be saying that we should be as eager to forgive as Lamech was to take vengeance. Just as Lamech wanted the punishment to far exceed the crime, we should want our forgiveness to far exceed the wrong done to us. We should be the exact opposite of Lamech, making our goal to forgive as extravagantly and completely as possible.[10]

I do think Tverberg is correct in asserting that was Jesus' intention because it was commonplace for Rabbis in Jesus' time (which he was) to use even a single unique word or phrase to hint back to a story and express their point more effectively. This teaching method was called *remez* (hint). Their culture was deeply literate in the Bible so these allusions to scripture would be more easily recognised. Jesus seems to be doing this to make his point here. But more significantly, this reference is the only of its kind. The phrase *shiv'im v'shiva* or seventy-seven times (70 x 7 = 490) is found only once in the Old Testament, which is this passage on Lamech. There is, however, an instance of the phrase *shiv'im shavu'im* ("seventy weeks") in Daniel 9:24-27, which means seventy weeks of seven years, adding up to the same total of (70 x 7 = 490) but in terms of years. The context of this passage is likewise one of judgement preceded by the grace period of seventy-sevens. Daniel is speaking of the timeframe of 483 years from the command to rebuild the Temple to the coming of the Messiah and his atoning death, and the final seven years of rule by the Antichrist (Cain's curse of seven) before God's final judgement. Reading the account above from Jasher with this additional context in mind reveals a profound revelation from the unwitting words and actions of Lamech. When Lamech vowed to avenge wrongdoers against himself seventy-sevenfold, he foreshadowed the grace period of 490 years given to those who wrong God in unbelief and ungodliness. With the death of Cain at the hands of his ungodly descendants, we now see a double

---

[10] Ibid.

fulfilment of God's judgement. Firstly, judgement unto Cain upon completion (seven) of God's promise of seven generations of time to re-join the godly line through repentance. Secondly, and most importantly, the coming judgement upon all of man (Cain is firstborn man personified, Abel is born again (second born) in Christ personified) to come after the final seven of the 490 years, as prophesied by Daniel (DAN. 9:24-27). In offering seventy-sevenfold opportunities to Lamech and his line to repent and be reconciled to Him, God reveals His willingness to forgive rather than avenge. Of utmost importance to all is that God's mercifulness has to be met with His righteous judgement, and it will come seven years from the coming of the Antichrist, at the conclusion of the *shiv'im shavu'im*. Just as God judged the kings of Israel for stubbornness and rebellion (1 SAM. 15:23), so he will to that portion of mankind who persists in this attitude of the line of Cain. When this judgement ("day of the Lord") comes after the completed 490 years, the six special messianic requirements will be fulfilled, and the messianic age of peace will be ushered in (DAN. 9:24). These requirements are:

1. Finish *the* transgression.
2. Make an end of sins.
3. Make reconciliation for iniquity.
4. Bring everlasting righteousness.
5. Seal up vision and prophecy.
6. Anoint the Most Holy.

That which follows is the permanent separation of the godly from the ungodly. The death, burial, and resurrection of the Messiah has made these six acts and subsequent separation possible, for the judgement of guilty was pronounced at the cross, but the execution of the sentence requires his return as righteous king to inflict the vengeance of God (ISA. 61:2; 2 THESS. 1:7-9).

Tubal-Cain

Tubal-Cain was the son of Lamech and "an instructor of every artificer of brass and iron" (GEN. 4:22). This is the only mention of Tubal-Cain in canonical scripture. Josephus added that Tubal-Cain "exceeded all men in strength, and was very expert and famous in martial performances.[11] In reference to the fifth-century midrash on ancient oral teachings, Genesis Rabbah, the famous Rabbi Rashi noted how Tubal-Cain "refined and improved the work of Cain by providing weapons for murderers."[12]

Tubal-Cain is greatly esteemed in occult literature, particularly so in Freemasonry. This is no surprise considering that Tubal-Cain is the original artificer and blacksmith. He is elevated by the Freemasons to the status of "God of the smiths and working tools" and the "Great Hierophant and High Priest of Commerce, War and Materialism."[13] The occultists have in mind a Messiah figure from the root of Tubal-Cain and his ancestor Cain who will stamp out the undesirables—those who impede the process of unity. The victims of their assault are not to be confused with the wicked who propagate perpetual evil on earth, but the forces of good who are trying to stamp that evil out. These occult sources claim it is Tubal-Cain who will return to "judge between the nations and cause men to beat their swords into ploughshares, and learn war no more" (ISA. 2:4; JOEL 3:9-10). The fulfilment of this prophecy is usually reserved for Jesus the Messiah for when he returns in judgement. In this vein, the promise from Jesus that he will return not "to bring peace, but a sword" is ascribed to Tubal-Cain (MATT. 10:34). He is positioned as the force of judgement over the world, not Jesus. Tubal-Cain is considered the prototype or forerunner of Hiram Abiff, the master builder and metalworker of Solomon's Temple who appears in the most important ritual ceremony for the highest Masonic Degree, the *Third Degree*. The Bible refers to both figures as "craftsmen in bronze" using the same Hebrew words, *choresh*

---

[11] Josephus, "Antiquities of the Jews," 1.60.

[12] Rashi on Genesis 4:22; Genesis Rabbah 23:3.

[13] Steiner, *The Temple Legend,* lecture 7.

nechosheth (GEN. 4:22; 1 KGS. 7:14). Tubal-Cain was the founder of the craft in which Hiram Abiff excelled, and he was the direct link between the two earliest pillars and those of Solomon's Temple.[14]

According to Freemason Rudolf Steiner, "the legend of Hiram Abiff forms the basis for the whole of Freemasonry" as an expression of its secrecy and its tendencies.[15] As recorded in the book on Masonic initiation rituals called *Masonic Ritual and Monitor*, the password used in the Hiram Abiff ritual just so happens to be "Tubal-Cain."[16] This ritual is said to derive from the earliest legend incorporated in the *Old Charges*, the foundational documents for the history of Masonry and its biblical origins. The legend is as follows:

> *The four children of Lamech, fearing that the world was to be destroyed by fire or flood, 'took counsel together' and decided to inscribe 'all the sciences' that they had founded, upon two pillars, one of marble and the other of clay-brick, because the one would not burn and the other would not sink in water ... These two pillars, not Solomon's, were the earliest pillars in the legendary history of the Craft and our story then goes on to recount how the world was saved in Noah's flood and how the science of masonry traveled from the east through Egypt into Europe and was finally established in England.[17]*

Another Masonic legend connecting the two fathers of Freemasonry occurs during the building of the First Temple. According to the legend, Hiram Abiff tried to cast a molten sea of bronze inside the Temple for his masterpiece work. Three jealous craftsmen conspired to undermine the project because he refused to divulge the Master Word which protected the secrets of the

---

14 Carr, *The Freemason at Work*, 169-171.

15 Steiner, *The Temple Legend,* lecture 7.

16 Duncan, *Duncan's Masonic Ritual and Monitor*, 87-90.

17 Carr, *The Freemason at Work*, 169-171.

Freemason craft. Hiram Abiff struggled to arrest the flow of the molten cast and as it poured out to the surroundings, the voice of Tubal-Cain called out to him. Tubal-Cain told him to plunge into the sea of fire to reach "the center of the earth where fire has its origin." There Hiram Abiff met Tubal-Cain and his ancestor Cain, who "irradiated with the brightness of Lucifer, the angel of light." This was the domain of Lucifer, where the "tyrannous envy of Adonai ceases" and all can "taste the fruit of the tree of knowledge."

> *Tubal-Cain introduced Hiram into the sanctuary of fire, where he expounded to him the weakness of Adonai [God] and the base position of that god ... Hiram was led into the presence of the author of his race, Cain. The angel of light that begat Cain was reflected in the beauty of this son of love, whose noble and generous mind roused the envy of Adonai. Cain related to Hiram his experiences, sufferings, and misfortunes, brought upon him by the implacable Adonai. Presently he heard the voice of him who was the offspring of Tubal-Cain and his sister Naamah: "A son shall born unto thee whom thou shalt indeed not see, but whose numerous descendants shall perpetuate thy race, which, superior to that of Adam, shall acquire the empire of the world; for many centuries they shall consecrate their courage and genius to the service of the ever ungrateful race of Adam, but at last the best shall become the strongest, and restore on the earth the worship of fire. Thy sons, invincible in thy name, shall destroy the power of kings, the ministers of the Adonai's tyranny."[18]*

Tubal-Cain initiated Hiram into the "Mystery of Fire" and gave him a hammer with the power to turn all things from chaos to order. Hiram Abiff returned to the surface of the earth, and with

---

[18] Steiner, *The Temple Legend,* lecture 7.

the power of Tubal-Cain's hammer, tamed the molten sea, his crowning achievement.[19]

Tubal-Cain, the "God of smiths," who turns chaos into order with his hammer, was later paralleled by the Roman god Vulcan, the god of fire, including metalworking and the forge, who is similarly depicted with a blacksmith's hammer:

> *That Tubal Cain gave first occasion to the name and worship of Vulcan been very probably conceived, both from the very great affinity of the names, and that Tubal Cain is expressly mentioned to be an instructor of every artificer in brass and iron; and as near relation as Apollo had to Vulcan, Jubal had to Tubal Cain, who was the inventor of music, or the father of all such as handle the harp and organ, which the Greeks attribute to Apollo.[20]*

Seth, and the Plan of Genetic Corruption

Seth was the third son of Adam and Eve. Eve named him Seth, meaning *appointed*, for Eve knew Seth was appointed by God to propagate the godly line. "God has appointed another seed for me instead of Abel, whom Cain killed" said Eve (GEN. 4:25). The replacement of the godly Abel with Seth restored the possibility for Jesus, the godly seed of the woman, to be born. To frustrate these plans of salvation for man, and judgement for himself, Lucifer devised plans to corrupt the spiritual and biological makeup of the Sethites.

It is said that when Seth had his son Enos, "then men began to call upon the name of the Lord" (GEN. 4:26). The significance of this verse is worth unpacking fully. The Hebrew word translated *began* in this text is *chalal*, which in some contexts is rendered as *profane*. The Hebrew sages through the centuries translated *chalal* in this text as *profane and defile*, in the sense of either

---

[19] Ibid., lecture 5.

[20] Oliver, *The Historical Landmarks and Other Evidences of Freemasonry, Explained*, 205.

ceasing to honour the Most High or ascribing his name to idolatrous worship. In the *Targum of Jonathan*, it is said that it was the generation starting from Enos who "began to err, and to make themselves idols, and surnamed their idols by the name of the Word of the Lord."[21] If this interpretation of chalal as profane or defile was correct, clearly this would indicate that the serpent was seeking a complete rejection of the Most High by the sons of Adam to cut off the promised seed. Without a means for the seed to emerge, there is obviously no Messiah to strike the final blow to the serpent's head.

Contrary to the sages, many scholars today render it as *begun* in the sense of *to begin* calling on the name of God. The two interpretations we are left with are diametrically opposed. Either there was a turning toward worship or there was a turning away from it. Since just a few generations later God destroyed the world by flood due to the wickedness of man, I am inclined to believe the sages were correct in their understanding.

A faithful remnant from the line of Seth would continue to propagate the godly line, but not without difficulty. Josephus had much to say about the sons of Seth in his *Antiquities of the Jews*:

> *Now this posterity of Seth continued to esteem God as the Lord of the universe, and to have an entire regard to virtue, for seven generations; but in process of time they were perverted and forsook the practices of their forefathers; and did neither pay those honors to God which were appointed them, nor had they any concern to do justice towards men. But for what degree of zeal, they had formerly shown for virtue, they now showed by their actions a double degree of wickedness, whereby they made God to be their enemy. For many angels of God accompanied with women, and begat sons that proved unjust, and despisers of all that was good, on account of the confidence they had in their own strength; for the*

---

[21] Targum Jonathan on Genesis 4:26b.

> *tradition is, that these men did what resembled the acts of those whom the Grecians call giants.*[22]

The serpent initiated another major offensive to corrupt the godly seed of the Sethites to transform them into a people whose disposition was only towards sin and rebellion against God:

> *Now it came about, when mankind began to multiply on the face of the land, and daughters were born to them, that the sons of God saw that the daughters of mankind were beautiful; and they took wives for themselves, whomever they chose. Then the Lord said, "My Spirit will not remain with man forever, because he is also flesh; nevertheless his days shall be 120 years." The Nephilim were on the earth in those days, and also afterward, when the sons of God came in to the daughters of mankind, and they bore children to them. Those were the mighty men who were of old, men of renown (Gen. 6:1-4 NASB).*

The plan was to render the biological profile of the Sethites ungodly. If this could be achieved, the seed of the woman could never be born. Neither he, nor his potential parents, would be able or willing to walk in step with God and fulfil His plan of salvation. The rebel angels would come out as victors in the war against God. The plan was for the sons of God, the fallen angels, to descend to earth and interbreed with human women (GEN. 6:1-7; 1 ENO. 1-36; JUB. 5-7). The offspring from these forbidden relationships were called *Nephilim* or giants, and they were utterly wicked by nature and capable only of evil (GEN. 6:4-7; NUM. 13:31-33).

Some argue for a purely naturalistic interpretation of this admittedly difficult passage, positing that these sons of God were not fallen angels, but the godly sons of Seth who profaned themselves by having sexual relations with "the daughters of

---

[22] Josephus, "Antiquities of the Jews," 1.72.

men," the ungodly offspring of Cain. Their giant offspring, they say, is not a physical designation, but merely a description of natural prowess or spiritual aptitude. The crucial issue is that these descendants were simply sons of Seth, and therefore sons of Adam. No one was a son of God. As we know, Adam was a son of God before the fall, a direct supernatural creation equal with the angels (LUKE 3:38), but after the transgression all of mankind lost their sonship of God. The restoration of this sonship was precisely why the seed of the woman, the only son of God had to enter the realm of man in the first place (JOHN 3:16; 1 JOHN 3:2-3; 5:1; LUKE 6:35; 20:34-36; GAL. 3:26; ROM. 8:14-19; EPH. 1:5; 2 COR. 6:18).

> *But as many as received him, to them gave he power to become the sons of God, even to them that believe on his name: Which were born, not of blood, nor of the will of the flesh, nor of the will of man, but of God (John 1:12-13 KJV).*

Jesus himself told us how those who resurrect to eternal life are like "angels of God in heaven," and that they are "equal to the angels and are sons of God" (LUKE 20:34-36; MATT. 22:29-30). The equivalency of the two phrases connotes an angelic interpretation of the Genesis usage of "the sons of God."

Another obvious refutation is how the phrase "sons of God" is interchanged with "angels of God" in numerous texts. In the Genesis 6:4 passage, the Septuagint manuscript *Codex Alexandrinus*, considered one of the oldest and best manuscripts of the Bible, renders the phrase as "the angels of God." In the book of Job, the only other usage of the phrase in the OT, the "sons of God" are gathered before the Lord in a divine council, and Satan is among them (JOB 1:6-7; 2:1-2; 38:7). The non-canonical books of Enoch, Jubilees, and the historical works of Josephus, all interpret the sons of God in this Nephilim context to be angels (1 ENO. 7:2; JUB. 5:1-2).[23] The Dead Seas Scroll document *4Q266* also mentions how

---

[23] Ibid.

the sons of God were "the Watchers of the heavens" and how their offspring were the size and stature of cedar trees and mountains.[24]

For those who maintain the Sethite connection, how would a union between Sethites and ungodly women produce a hybrid race of giants of exceptional size, given over to wickedness and immorality and occult arts? There is no natural reason to explain this transformation, but we know such giants existed on the earth even after the flood (NUM. 13:22-33; DEUT. 1:28; 2:10-3:14; 9:2; JOSH. 12:4-5; 13:10-12; 1 SAM. 17:4-7). We will explore the biblical passages surrounding these giants in the following section.

Nephilim Testimony of Enoch and Jubilees

The book of Enoch, specifically the book of the Watchers, provides extensive background on these forbidden affairs by angels of God, not men (1 ENO. 1-37).[25] While the book is not considered canonical, it is frequently referenced in the New Testament (JUDE 1:4, 6, 13–15; 2 PET. 2:4; 3:13; JOHN 7:38) and is well-regarded by both Jews and Christians. In the Epistle of Jude in the New Testament, Enoch is quoted and endorsed directly for his deeper writings on the angelic incursion (JUDE 1:6, 14-15; 1 ENO. 1:9). Enoch recounted that two hundred rebellious angels descended from the heavenly realm to Mount Hermon to hatch this wicked plan on earth (1 ENO. 6). These fallen angels assumed the form of humans to engage in sexual activity with human women and marry them freely (GEN. 6:1-2). Jesus revealed that the angels in heaven do not marry (MATT. 22:30; LUKE 20:34-36), but these rebel angels violated that principle for the ultimate purpose of eliminating the godly seed. They corrupted their Nephilim offspring with wicked and forbidden knowledge (1

---

[24] Dead Sea Scroll fragment 4Q266 (4QDamascus Documenta), frag. 2 col. II, 15–21, DSSSE 1:585).

[25] The essay "They Revealed Secrets to Their Wives': The Transmission of Magical Knowledge in 1 Enoch" by Rebecca Lesses highlights some very interesting insights into the events during the pre-flood period and their ongoing ramifications through history. Lesses, "The Transmission of Magical Knowledge in 1 Enoch," *With Letters of Light*, 196-222, https://www.marquette.edu/maqom/letters123.pdf#page=205.

ENO. 7-9, 13, 16) and led them to "afflict, oppress, destroy, attack, do battle, and work destruction on the earth" (1 ENO. 15:10-12).

The book of Jubilees, another highly regarded non-canonical book, corroborated the Enochic elaboration of the Genesis account and noted how the wicked Nephilim "sinned against the beasts and birds, and all that moved and walked on the earth" (JUB. 4:28-29; 5:1-15; 7:25-31). This was totally contrary to the laws of God. Clear boundaries were established between angels and humans, and humans and animals. Without exception, reproduction was reserved for two of like kind (GEN. 1:21, 24-25). The ancient Rabbis pointed out how crossbreeding between the species angered God into sending the great deluge upon the earth. In the Talmud and the Midrash *Tanchuma*, the corruption of all flesh (GEN. 6:12) applied not simply to the hybridization of man, but of all living creatures.[26] Rabbi Nevins noted how the "orderly procession of animals into the ark 'two by two' emphasizes species differentiation ... a priority of the Creator."[27]

The New Testament books 1 and 2 Peter, as well as Jude, give witness to the Enochian idea of these fallen angels from "the days of Noah" being cast as prisoners in the abyss until the day of judgement (1 PET. 3:18-22; 2 PET. 2:4-10; JUDE 5-7, 14-15; JUB. 10:8-19).

Confirmation by Jesus

Jesus, being a Rabbi himself, would have been familiar with the writings on the angelic incursion from the books of Enoch, Jasher and Jubilees. The angels were said to have descended upon Mount Hermon which was a location of spiritual significance for pagans and Jews alike. Mount Hermon was at one time a sacred and holy mountain for worshippers of the supreme Canaanite god El or Baal (JUDG. 3:3; 1 CHR. 5:23; JOSH. 11:17; 13:5). It was here that El supposedly held council with his consort Asherah (Athirat) and

---

[26] Sanhedrin 108a:11; Midrash Tanchuma, Noach 12:4.

[27] Nevins, "Noah 5775: Species Purity and the Great flood," *Rabbi Danny Nevins,* https://rabbinevins.com/2014/10/22/noah-5775-species-purity-and-the-great-flood/.

their seventy sons. There is much biblical testimony of Israel falling into false worship of "the Baals and Asherahs" (JUDG. 2:13; 3:7; 10:6). By the time of Jesus, the surrounding area of Caesarea Philippi was collectively referred to as the "gates of hell," an allusion to the demonic authority that resided there. Etchings of this were found in a cave at the base of the mountain called the cave of Pan. The cave was a popular pagan site for the worship of the goat-footed Greek god Pan, a fertility god traceable to the Phoenician sun god Baal (take note now of this theme of Baal).[28]

Jesus deliberately took his disciples to Caesarea Philippi, the city at the foot of Mount Hermon, "to destroy the works of the devil" which dwelt there (1 JOHN 3:8). He came to the place most venerated by the followers of Satan to declare the days of their wretched works on earth were numbered. By confronting the Satanic forces of spiritual oppression, his disciples were to come to a greater understanding of the nature of their mission. Jesus sent his disciples there to preach the gospel, heal the sick and most importantly, to cast out demons.

The book of Jubilees mentions how the spirits of the Nephilim turned into evil spirits on earth to lead people astray and destroy them (JUB. 10:1-2). I believe these demonic spirits were the Nephilim, not the fallen angels themselves, and they were drawn to the bodies of humans for habitation out of internal conflict with their cursed hybridized nature. At Satan's request, God supposedly allowed one-tenth of them to escape their shackles in prison so Satan could continue to exercise his will over man (JUB. 10:7-19). This was the means by which Satan could test the faithfulness of man to God by tempting them into idolatry. This extra-biblical account could be purely speculative, but it is interesting to consider within the biblical framework.

It was not until Jesus and his disciples were there in Caesarea Philippi that he probed his disciples on the question of his divinity. I believe this was intentional. In the place of the fallen sons of God,

---

[28] Prasch, "Nephilim, Pan and Pontifex Maximus," *Moriel TV*, July 31, 2017, video, 53:49, https://youtu.be/Vieoe6hoUEE.

he revealed himself as *the son* of God. It was Peter who stepped forward and declared "you are the Messiah the son of the Living God" (MATT. 16:15-16; MARK 8:29; LUKE 9:20). That Peter called Jesus the son of the *living* God indicated he was aware of the false gods surrounding the area—those that were *dead*. Furthermore, to recognise him as the son of God, not as the son of man, was significant. The messianic expectation until this point was of a son of man, as per the designation from Daniel (DAN 7:13-14). The excursion to Mount Hermon must have been a revelatory awakening for Peter, and God knew he was fit to receive the revelation (MATT. 16:17). Jesus thereby declared that "on this rock I will build my church, and the gates of Hades shall not prevail against it" (MATT. 16:17-19). Jesus was making a statement to two audiences at once. First to the men he came to save, and secondly, to the rebellious angels he came to condemn. The very place that embodied all that was evil in the sight of God, the realm of Satan, was to become the realm of God. The metaphor here is that the rock which Jesus was to build the Church on top of was quite literally in their sight, it was the cave of Pan, the very "gates of Hades" that symbolised Satanic authority. The saints were given the "keys of the kingdom of heaven" to tread underfoot the kingdom of Satan (MATT. 16:19). The promise God gave to Abraham that his seed (Jesus) shall possess the gate of his enemies had been realised (GEN. 22:15-18).

With this new divine understanding of Jesus, Jesus found it appropriate to reveal to them how he will be rejected and killed but will rise on the third day (MATT. 16:21-23). Under the direct control of Satan, Peter was compelled to cry out "Lord this shall never be" to which Jesus rebuked with, "get behind me Satan!" Satan knew that Jesus was close to saving mankind and condemning the forces of evil. Jesus was signaling to the fallen principalities and powers of darkness on their earthly base that the Church he established in their ungodly domain would triumph (1 COR. 15:55-57). Remember that it was not Satan who led Jesus to the cross, but Jesus who led Satan there (more on this in the companion book "Seed of God: Jesus Christ"). The seventy followers Jesus sent out in his name (remember how El and his seventy sons dwelled on Mount Hermon?) returned to him amazed that even the demons were subject to them in his name, to which Jesus replied that he saw "Satan fall like lightning from heaven" (LUKE 10:17-19). The power of the Church that Jesus was establishing alarmed Satan greatly, for he knew his time of dominion was fleeting.

Six days later Jesus walked to the top of Mount Hermon to proclaim his sonship of God to his disciples, and to the fallen sons of God who first landed there (MATT. 17:1-9; MARK 9:2-8; LUKE 9:28-36). Jesus transfigured atop the "gates of hell" and shone with the radiant light of God's presence. The voice of God spoke out to the disciples and said, "this is My Son, My Chosen One; listen to Him!" (MATT. 17:5; MARK 9:7; LUKE 9:35). In the midst of this transformative experience, the disciples saw Jesus next to Moses and Elijah, the two witnesses to return in the end days to condemn these fallen angels. He was talking to them, and to the demonic forces, once again on the subject of his salvific death.

Adam as the first son of God enjoyed this body of light before the fall but after the separation the light of God dissipated from his body and he realised he was naked.[29] Consequently, all of man became separated from God in a spiritual and physical sense (GEN 3:7-8). The transfiguration of Christ indicated that a second man had been born in the image of God. The fall had been reversed. Through him, fallen mankind could be restored as sons of God as a second man.[30]

---

[29] Hamp, "Adam's Biophotons and Future Bodies of Light," chap. 2 in *Corrupting the Image.*

[30] Barry Britnell of the website Exploring Bible Lands connected Mount Hermon to the mountain in which Jesus transfigured: "Matthew and Mark describe the location as "a high mountain" (Matt. 17:1; Mark 9:2), and Luke refers to it as "the mountain" with a definite article (Luke 9:28). If they were in the region of Caesarea Philippi and they went up a high mountain ... indeed the most noteworthy mountain in the area ... then it is not difficult to figure out which mountain was intended"
https://www.exploringbiblelands.com/journal/2012/07/12/mount-hermon-and-caesarea-philippi.

The Corrupted Sons of Ham

With the flood, God wiped the wicked old world away so life could start anew. The task of propagating life throughout the world was given to Noah and his family for remaining faithful to God before the flood. Although the giants had been destroyed in the flood and the two-hundred rebel angels cast into the abyss, their DNA strain along with their spiritual descendants (demons) had not. They would continue to exercise their spiritual influence over the new humanity that was disembarking the ark to repopulate the earth.

After the ark settled on dry ground, Noah and his family went out and offered sacrifice to God in thanks. We are then told about Noah getting drunk on wine and being found naked in his tent by his son, Ham (GEN. 9:20-27). Noah responded by placing a curse upon the son of Ham, Canaan, declaring that Canaan would become a servant to his uncles Shem and Japheth. The peculiarity of this event raises several questions. For what reason would Noah, who had acted foolishly by getting drunk and lying naked, pronounce a curse upon someone else? Furthermore, why curse Canaan, the son of Ham, who is not to blame for this dilemma?

The way Josephus described this story implied that Ham brought shame upon his father because "he came laughing" to his brothers after catching him in this unseemly manner.[31] This small detail was not explicitly mentioned in the Biblical account, but it makes sense considering the stark contrast in the conduct of his brothers who were said to have walked backwards into the tent to cover their father gracefully (GEN. 9:22-23). Josephus claimed that Noah did not curse Ham "by reason of his nearness in blood but cursed his prosperity" in his place.

Another perspective put forth in the book of Jubilees contends that Canaan took the land inheritance that was owed to his brother Shem who God favoured:

And Canaan saw the land of Lebanon to the river of Egypt, that it was very good, and he went not into the

---

[31] Josephus, "Antiquities of the Jews," 1.140.

47

land of his inheritance to the west (that is to) the sea, and he dwelt in the land of Lebanon ... and Ham, his father, and Cush and Mizraim his brothers said unto him: 'Thou hast settled in a land which is not thine, and which did not fall to us by lot: do not do so; for if thou dost do so, thou and thy sons will fall in the land and (be) accursed through sedition; for by sedition ye have settled, and by sedition will thy children fall, and thou shalt be rooted out for ever. Dwell not in the dwelling of Shem; for to Shem and to his sons did it come by their lot. Cursed art thou, and cursed shalt thou be beyond all the sons of Noah, by the curse by which we bound ourselves by an oath in the presence of the holy judge, and in the presence of Noah our father.' But he did not hearken unto them, and dwelt in the land of Lebanon from Hamath to the entering of Egypt, he and his sons until this day. And for this reason that land is named Canaan (Jub. 10:29-34).

I believe this curse was prophesied under the anointing of the Holy Spirit because of the inevitable conflict between the Canaanites and the Jews. The land of Canaan is within the territory of the promised land given unto the Jews. It was not Noah, but the Holy Spirit, who revealed Canaan was to be a servant of servants under both Shem and Japheth. In this view, "praise be to the Lord, the God of Shem" indicates that God is with the line of Shem. We know from the genealogy of Jesus that he traces his descent back through Shem (not Ham or Japheth) to Adam (LUKE 3:23-38). Canaan subject to the rule of Shem is thus a picture of the ungodly line subject to the rule of the godly line under Jesus Christ, the descendent of Shem and adversary of the Canaanites. This contentious plot of land is destined for God and His people.

Another possible line of questioning is whether the curse on Canaan could have been because Noah or God knew he was tainted with Nephilim blood and inherited their DNA strain. Noah was said to be "a just man, perfect in his generation" who walked with God and found grace in his eyes (GEN. 6:9). The conventional understanding of the terms just and perfect is that they both describe the same thing, righteousness before God. Not sinlessness, indeed none but Jesus can accept this honour, but faithful and upstanding in the ways of God. The question is whether the redundancy is simply to emphasise the godliness of Noah, or if the usage of perfect denotes his pure physical makeup, unblemished by the Nephilim interference? What would it look like to be perfect "in his generation," which was thoroughly infested with Nephilim? Why would God choose Noah from his generation to save through the flood?

However, the issue of the Nephilim presents a troubling reality because: "the Nephilim were on the earth in those days, and also afterward," speaking of their postdiluvian existence (GEN. 6:4). There were eight people on the ark, the remainder of which were the wives of Noah's sons (GEN. 6:18; 1 PET. 3:20). Since the flood wiped the world of the Nephilim (GEN. 6:13, 17), we can deduce that one or more of the wives of Noah's sons were latent carriers of the Nephilim strain. We can confidently exempt Noah, his wife, and his son Shem, for this is the uncontaminated line which brought about Jesus Christ, the seed of the woman (GEN. 3:15). From what I can gather, this may have been the case for the wife of Ham. I will soon explain my reasoning, but first I will present more evidence for the postdiluvian existence of the Nephilim.

Postdiluvian Existence of Nephilim

During the time of Joshua when the Israelites were about to enter the promised land, spies went into the land of Canaan and sighted Nephilim (giants) there which made them look "as grasshoppers in their sight" (NUM. 13:33). This land which God promised to the progeny of Abraham by oath is the land occupied by the descendants of Canaan, the son of Ham. The presence of Nephilim in the land settled by Canaan could point to him as its origin, and to frustrate the land promises of God aligns perfectly with the ungodly intentions of their fallen angel ancestors.[32]

Image 2.1 – Post-flood tribes of giants

POST-FLOOD GIANTS	REFERENCES
Anakim	Num. 13:33
Emin	Deut. 2:10-11
Zuzim	Deut. 2:20
Amorites	Amos. 2:9-10
Rephaites	Deut. 2:11; 20-22; 3:11-13; Josh. 12:4-5; 13:10-13
Goliath and Giants from Gath	1 Sam. 17:4-7; 2 Sam. 21:15-22; 1 Chr. 20:4-8

Careful research of history will show that the bones of giants have been found all over the earth. As far back as the fifth century BC, we have records of giant remains being found. The work written in 430 BC which founded the field of history in the Western world, *Histories* by Herodotus, tells of the discovery of a giant measuring twelve feet long.[33]

Later in the first century AD, first it was Josephus who mentioned that the bones of the Amorite giants were still on display, and described them as having "bodies so large, and countenances so entirely different from other men."[34] Secondly, in the encyclopedic *Naturalis Historia* ("Natural History"), Pliny the Elder relayed that a body forty-six cubits in height (sixty-eight feet) was found on the island of Crete following an earthquake. Pliny thought that this was evidence that the men of old were of a far greater physical stature than men in his day, and mentioned

---

[32] For an exhaustive analysis of the different traditions on the Nephilim or giants, please consult the following academic work: Stuckenbruck, "The 'Angels' and 'Giants' of Genesis 6:1-4 in Second and Third Century BCE Jewish Interpretation: Reflections on the Posture of Early Apocalyptic Traditions," 354-377.

[33] Herodotus, *Histories*, 1.68.

[34] Josephus, "Antiquities of the Jews," 5.125.

how the poet Homer complained of the same thing a thousand years prior.[35]

In the third century, Flavius Philostratus in *Heroicus* ("On Heroes") noted the discovery of many giant skeletons throughout the Greek world, many of which were still viewable for the public.[36] Gaius Julius Solinus similarly recorded in *Polyhistor* how it was still commonplace for people to discover these bones:

> *It is said that the soldiery of heaven fought there [Phlegra or Pallene] with the giants ... evidence of divine wars perseveres into this age. If at any time ... the torrents become swollen with rain, and they break their banks with the increased weight of water, throwing themselves into the plain, bones are said to be even now uncovered ... These bones are in the form of human bones, but larger. Because of their immense size, it is said that they are from the bodies of that monstrous army.*[37]

Reports on the presence of giants on earth have persisted through the ages right up to the present day. Archaeological evidence has supposedly been found to support this idea, at least according to Hugh Newman, the author of "Giants on Record." Newman claimed in an interview with newspaper Desert Sun that bones from these giants have been dug up by archaeologists as far as North America, but researcher access to the bones and DNA is strictly prohibited "because of the NAGPRA Act – the Native American Grave Protection and Repatriation Act."[38] He maintains that he does not personally "think they're alien-human hybrids or

---

[35] Pliny, *Natural History*, 7.16.

[36] Philostratus, *On Heroes*, 8.3-16.

[37] Solinus, *Polyhistor*, 9.6, https://topostext.org/work/747.

[38] Fessier, "Annunaki, Nephilim and Denisovans? Contact in Desert explores ancient giants," *Desert Sun*, https://www.desertsun.com/story/life/entertainment/people/brucefessierentertainment/2019/05/23/annunaki-nephilim-and-denisovans-contact-desert-explores-ancient-giants/3700717002/.

anything like that," but is intrigued by the Native American oral legends about "interbreeding with the star people" which produced giants. The parallel to the Biblical story is remarkable, and it is only one of many of the world cultures that have passed down a flood story.[39]

You will find many more such statements through the centuries attesting to this union between the angelic and earthly realms. Another theory is that the wife of Noah died sometime before the flood and that Noah remarried with a woman from the line of Cain who was tainted with Nephilim DNA. When Ham entered his father Noah's tent and noticed him and his stepmother drunk and asleep, it is thought that Ham took sexual liberty with his stepmother and together they produced hybrid offspring. Noah, under the direct anointing of the Holy Spirit, responded by pronouncing a curse on the unborn Nephilim son of this act of fornication to be called Canaan (Gen. 9:18-29). This course of events would vindicate Noah for his strange curse on Canaan.

The question becomes whether all the sons of Ham were corrupted by the way of Ham's wife, or only Canaan, by the way of Noah's new wife, if he did indeed have a new wife. As we proceed down the ungodly line with the sons of Ham, the character and actions of these sons are shown to be such that the likelihood of Canaan being the only corrupted one is low. Therefore, from this point forward, I shall investigate the evidence for this perspective, starting with Ham's youngest son, Canaan.

Canaan

Canaan, the son of Ham, begat all the families who came to occupy the land called by his name, collectively termed the Canaanites (Gen. 10:15-18). Some of these tribes eventually established the main adversarial kingdoms to the Israelites, such as the Amorites that

---

[39] Cultures all across the world have developed stories and folklore on a singular world flood event independently of each other. For deeper reading on this subject, a good starting point is the following article from *The Metropolitan Museum of Art*: https://www.metmuseum.org/toah/hd/flod/hd_flod.htm.

set up the First Babylonian Empire and forced Marduk worship. This area of land is also known as the Levant, which covered Phoenicia, Philistia, Israel, and other nations crucial to salvation history. This was the promised land allotted to Abraham and his descendants by the oath of God but was claimed by the Canaanites while the Hebrews were enslaved in Egypt (GEN. 12:5-7; 13:14-18; 15:13-21; 17:3-10). At one time it was co-habited by the Anakim, who were known to be giants who engendered fear in the hearts of the Israelites. The son of Canaan, Sidon, was the founder of the city of Sidon or Zidon, the original metropolis of Phoenicia that quickly became identified as ground zero in the contest between the godly and ungodly lines (GEN. 10:15, 19; JOSH. 11:8; 19:28). As late as the first millennium BC, the inhabitants of the area known as Phoenicia still preferred to call themselves Canaanites.[40] It was the Greeks who insisted on calling them Phoenicians.

When the Israelites were delivered out of Egypt and entered the promised land, God instructed Israel under Joshua to totally eradicate this Nephilim hybrid and the seven godless nations which inhabited the land (DEUT. 7:1-2; 20:16-18). The God of Israel is hated for this unbending attitude against these peoples, but the survival of humanity, and the coming forth of its redeemer, depended on the Nephilim being eliminated. The wickedness of these peoples and the perpetual suffering they inflicted far outweighed that which was done unto them. The promised land had to be cleansed and purified in order to operate as a national priesthood to God and move along His salvation plan. The Israelites did not drive out all the Canaanites in the land, nor those in Sidon, and the ramifications were enormous. From our point of view, not knowing the outcome, the command seemed evil and incompatible with God's loving nature, but for God who knows everything (JOB 26:6; PSA. 90:8; HEB. 4:12-13) judgement was necessary to prevent greater evil (JUDG. 1:27-33). The promised land had not been set apart as holy as instructed by God, and the people fell into idolatry (JUDG. 10:6-16). Because of their transgressions, God could

---

[40] Drews, "Canaanites and Philistines," 48-49.

no longer dwell in their midst and they were quickly crushed by the same peoples of the gods they came to share. The pervasive influence of sin corrupted the nation and they never fully recovered. Even as one of the "better" kings Israel had, King Solomon indulged in this same idolatry (1 Kgs. 11). These malicious Canaanite neighbours which God called "painful briers and sharp thorns" are to be destroyed at the end of the age when God comes to sanctify His people (Ezek. 28:20-26; Joel 3:4-8).

Phut

Phut was the third son of Ham. Unique among the first patriarchs after Ham, no sons or grandsons of Phut are recorded in the Bible. However, the Book of Jasher gives the names of at least four sons, namely Gebul, Hadan, Benah and Adan (Jash. 7:12). The people of Phut were mercenaries in the armies of Egypt and Tyre, two of the most significant powers against the Most High (Jer. 46:9; Ezek. 27:10; 30:5). The warlike nature of the men of Phut is seen in scripture concerning the city of Tyre, where once again they appear to be operating as mercenaries in its defence: "Persia and Lud and Put were in your army as your men of war; they hung the shield and helmet in you; they gave you splendour" (Ezek. 27:10).

Phut is associated with the confederation of nations aligned with Gog of Magog's last days invasion of Israel (Ezek. 38:1-6). In fact, his descendants are to survive right to the end of the age to join the above confederation of non-Arab nations under a leader to be called Gog. This leader will be from the uttermost north of Israel and shall seek to take over the wealth and influence of Israel and dominate the whole Middle Eastern world.

Mizraim

Mizraim, translated as Egypt, was the second son of Ham. Mizraim begat Casluhim from whom came the Philistines and the Caphtorim (Gen. 10:14; 1 Chr. 1:12). As we know, God thought little enough of the Philistine descendants of Mizraim to destroy them (Jer. 47:4). The Philistines came from Caphtor, better known to us as Crete in Greece, or as the birthplace of the Greek gods, including Apollo, Artemis, and the king of the gods—Zeus, who were its protectors (JER. 47:4; AMOS 9:7). The name Zeus shares the meaning of Lucifer as light bearer, and to go further with the connection, a Greek myth states Aphrodite and Eros teamed up to cause Zeus to fall in love with a human named Europa. Not surprisingly she was a Phoenician princess and the personification of Europe (this connection will become clear in later chapters). Zeus disguised himself as a white bull to trick Europa into riding with him back to Crete where he raped and impregnated her.

Another legend located on the island of Crete is of the Minotaur, part man and part bull—in other words, a Nephilim. This reveals a joining of the angelic and the earthly that the creator previously destroyed the pre-flood world over. It seems to me that some of these myths and legends were alternate explanations offered by peoples seeing similar phenomena from the descendants of Mizraim.

Cush

Cush was the eldest son of Ham and is most notable for being the father of Nimrod (GEN. 10:6; 1 CHR. 1:8). The Cushites initially settled in the area known as Phoenicia and mingled with the Akkadians, which later became the nation Chaldea. The Chaldeans were later assimilated by the Babylonians, and they were famed for their practices of astrology and divination. As we know from Enoch, proficiency in the dark arts came from the ungodly influence of the fallen angels who taught their Nephilim children (1 ENO. 7:1; 8:3). These evil influences stretched as far as the Roman empire, as evidenced by the references to the Chaldeans by prominent Roman figures such as Cicero and Horace.[41]

The Cushites later moved to northern Africa and are associated with both sides of the Red Sea, Sudan, and Ethiopia. In the first-century, historian Josephus recorded that "the Ethiopians, over

---

[41] Cicero, On Divination, 1.2, 2.87; Cicero, "For Lucius Murena," 11.25; Horace, "Odes," 1.11.

whom he [Cush] reigned, are even at this day, both by themselves and by all men in Asia, called Cushites."[42] As with Phut (Libya), Cush (Ethiopia) is involved in Gog of Magog's last days invasion of Israel (EZEK. 38:1-6).

Nimrod the Prototype

Nimrod was the son of Cush, who "began to be a mighty one on the earth" as a "mighty hunter before the Lord" (GEN. 10:8-10; 1 CHR. 1:10). Some of the foremost Rabbis such as Rashi posit that Nimrod, whose name means to rebel, hunted not by the grace of God, but rather in rebellion against God.[43] "Nimrod ensnared people's minds with his speech and misled them to rebel against the Omnipresent."[44] Nimrod went "before the Lord" not in submission, but opposition, as a hunter not of animals, but of men. The Jerusalem Targum ("Targum Pseudo-Jonathan") emphasised that he hunted men by drawing them into his own rebellion against God—the express purpose of the Nephilim incursion into humanity.[45]

According to Josephus, Nimrod persuaded the people not to ascribe his mightiness to God, but to his own courage.[46] With his new recruits, he formed a kingdom in opposition to God at Babilu (Hebrew Babel), the first of its kind (GEN. 10:8-12; 11:1-9). It was the first organised one world order comprised of ungodly and worldly analogues for political, social, and religious order. The worldly spirit and influence of Nimrod and his kingdom served as a prototype for the many evil rulers opposed to God that came down the centuries. The ultimate manifestation will be realised by the Antichrist, who seeks to again unite *all* people and end the

---

[42] Josephus, "Antiquities of the Jews," 1.130.

[43] Refer to the commentaries of Rashi, Ramban and Targum Jonathan on Genesis 10:8-9.

[44] Rashi on Genesis 10:9 in reference to Genesis Rabbah 37:2, the midrash collection of ancient traditions.

[45] Jerusalem Targum on Genesis 10:9.

[46] Josephus, "Antiquities of the Jews," 1.113.

separation initiated at Babel. Josephus noted that Nimrod "gradually changed the government into tyranny, seeing no other way of turning men from the fear of God, but to bring them into a constant dependence on his power."[47] This matches the biblical account of the time of tribulation under the Antichrist when all of humanity are forcibly subjected to his every whim.

Jasher stated that, "All the nations and tongues heard of his [Nimrod] fame and gathered themselves to him ... and he became their lord and king" (JASH. 7:43-45; 9:20).[48] Jasher added that Nimrod was more wicked than all who came before him from the days of the flood. He caused the people to err from "the ways of the Lord" and openly rebel against Him (JASH. 7:46-47).

> *And all the princes of Nimrod and his great men took counsel together; Phut, Mizraim, Cush and Canaan with their families, and they said to each other, Come let us build ourselves a city and in it a strong tower, and its top reaching heaven, and we will make ourselves famed, so that we may reign upon the whole world (Jash. 9:21).*

The sons of Ham we discussed are shown here to be underlings of Nimrod in the great stand against God. Under the authority of Nimrod, all the peoples built the city and tower in Shinar to "war against Him [God] and to ascend into heaven" (GEN. 11:1-4; JASH. 9:23-31). In response, God confused the tongues of man so one could not understand the language of another and the rebellious project quickly disintegrated into chaos and disorder (GEN. 11:5-8; JASH. 9:32-34). The people began to scatter across the earth according to their language (GEN. 11:8-9; JASH. 9:35-37; 10; 11:1-10).[49] This was an important counter measure by God against the serpent line and its incessant attacks to render the godly line inoperative. I suspect that this was a strategy to keep the knowledge of the true seed in a more

---

[47] Ibid.

[48] Ibid., 1.115.

[49] Ibid., 1.115-1.120.

universal setting where it would be harder to dilute.

Counterfeiting the Redemptive Archetypes

Following the confusion of tongues and expulsion from Babel, Satan plotted on how to use the gains made in Babel to make a counter offensive to destroy the godly line, and thus the seed of the woman. One such plan was to counterfeit the archetypal prophecies God created and revealed in Genesis—the mother and child, and the dying and rising God—in a bid to muddy the waters of prophetic revelation so to speak. Enter the ancient mystery religions, or what can be rendered more colloquially as paganism. To Lucifer's credit, many today are inclined to believe in this counterfeit, and believe that the mystery religions are the real custodians of the pathway to Godhood. Since Christianity is a late arrival—and it did indeed begin some two-thousand years later— they claim it is therefore inauthentic and merely an inheritor of older ideas and traditions. To assess the veracity of this assertion, let us make our way through the history of these mystery religions.

Pagan sources take us back to Nimrod and Semiramis at Babel as the beginning of the mystery mother and child cult, presenting a template for understanding paganism and its outworking through history. Semiramis was both Nimrod's mother *and* his wife. From the beginning, the revered progenitors of the ancient mysteries are involved in an incestuous relationship, clearly demonstrating their immoral and ungodly roots. The parallels to the character of his spiritual father—the serpent—are abundantly clear. God told Noah after the flood that man was to spread out over the earth, but as king, Nimrod defied God's instruction by instead consolidating the people around his mighty city of Bavel (meaning gate of god). Nimrod was attempting to reach heaven by his own means. You could say Nimrod is the prototype for all consequent attempts of world government, all characterised by this circumvention of God and His Word out of arrogant self-aggrandisement and no fear towards divine authority.

After Nimrod died, Semiramis claimed him as the great sun god who miraculously impregnated her with his sun rays and gave her a son named Tammuz. By doing so, she was pre-empting the supernatural work of the Holy Spirit to come which brought about Jesus through his virgin mother, Mary. At her own death, she became known as the Queen of Heaven—a title many goddesses have claimed throughout history, and one that has been misapplied to Mary within Catholicism. Semiramis claimed Tammuz was the reincarnation of Nimrod, which played into the promise given by the serpent that "thou shall not surely die." This was another Luciferic attempt at undermining the salvation plan of God by pre-emptively forming a Triune Godhead. This ungodly trinity would see Nimrod the sun god as God the Father, Semiramis as the Holy Spirit (some Catholics call Mary the Queen of Heaven and the Holy Spirit), and Nimrod reincarnated in the body of Tammuz as Jesus, the Son.

To summarise, we have a trinity of Nimrod, Semiramis and Tammuz as being the source of the mother and child, and the dying and rising god and man motifs that characterise subsequent false religions all over the world. In actuality, the book of Genesis is the *true* origin of these motifs. Right near the beginning of time, Eve is promised a singular descendant to defeat the serpent and overturn the curse imposed on man following their transgression. For the original sin in the garden of Eden, God covered Adam and Eve with the animal skins as a temporary atonement for man. God was to personally manifest in the flesh as the promised seed and sacrifice himself as a man, for man, in a once and for all act of atonement for the curse of sin. As he would be "delivered over to death for our sins" he would be "raised to life for our justification" (ROM. 4:25). This motif of the dying and rising son of God was the first ever prophecy, the foundation of our faith and salvation. It was only logical that Lucifer counterfeit this foundational motif for his own purposes through his own prototype of the Antichrist, Nimrod. As for the mother and child archetype, Eve is promised a seed, but as women do not have the seed but the man, the text gives the first hint of the virgin birth of the promised seed (GEN.

3:15). As Mary conceived not through Joseph, but through the supernatural work of the Holy Spirit without recourse to sexual union, the promised seed of the godly line would be God manifesting in human flesh. This was far before the rise of Nimrod and Babel after the flood and the beginning of the mystery religions, who gained their revelations from the fallen angels who brought to mankind the occult knowledge.

What was Nimrod?

The ancient mystery religions have a counterfeit gospel in place to divert attention away from the genuine article. In this counterfeit, Nimrod is given a place of prominence and the Word of God concurs by placing emphasis on Nimrod attaining a unique standing among men. In scripture he is called *mighty* (gibbor), and again, a *mighty hunter* (gibbor sayid). The Nephilim, themselves mighty hunters of men, are also described as *mighty men* (hag-gibborim) (GEN. 6:4-6). The first mention of Nimrod in the Table of Nations after he is said to be begotten is that he *began* to be a mighty one (GEN. 10:8). The usage of began might imply that Nimrod began his life as one of the mighty Nephilim (gibborim). On its own the parallel of language seems speculative when we consider how mighty (gibbor) is used in many contexts which are innocuous, but in the Septuagint, the oldest surviving Greek translation of the Old Testament used by Jesus and the apostles, the word *giant* (Nephilim) is in the place of *gibbor* (mighty).

The ancient Greek historian Eupolemus recorded that there was a Nephilim presence at Babel during the building of the Tower of Babel:

> *The city Babylon was first founded by those who escaped from the Deluge; and that they were giants, and built the tower renowned in history. But when this had been overthrown by the act of God, the giants were dispersed over the whole earth ... Abraham traced back his origin to the giants, and that they dwelling in Babylonia were destroyed by the gods for their impiety; but that one of*

them, named Belus, escaped death and settled in Babylon, and lived in a tower which he had built, and which was called Belus from the Belus who built it.[50]

There is another non-biblical perspective in the fourth-century historical compilation, the *History of Armenia*. In Armenian tradition, Nimrod is remembered as a giant who enlisted the aid of other giants to assist in the building of the Tower of Babel.[51]

There is, however, another way of interpreting these troublesome passages which does not involve the Nephilim. The more obvious implication of how Nimrod *began* to be a mighty one (GEN. 10:8) is that he experienced a transformation in strength. The book of Jasher claimed the source of his mightiness was the temporary garments of salvation which God covered Adam and Eve with after the fall (JASH. 7:24-30; GEN. 3:21). Jasher recorded that these same garments were passed down the generations and survived the flood with Noah. When Ham dishonoured his naked father Noah and bore the strange curses, according to Jasher, it was because Ham stole these God-given garments for himself (JASH. 7:27). If this is the case, it could explain the harsh response Noah had towards Ham and his progeny with the placement of the curse. The garments eventually landed in the hands of the mighty hunter Nimrod through his father Cush, the son of Ham (JASH. 7:28-29). "Nimrod became strong when he put on the garments" and easily conquered all the surrounding peoples (JASH. 7:30-42; 27:10). Rabbi Jehudah, as quoted in the midrash *Pirkei DeRabbi Eliezer*, agreed with the account of Jasher, and said:

> *All beasts, animals, and birds, when they saw the coats, came and prostrated themselves before him [Nimrod]. The sons of men thought that this (was due) to the power*

---

[50] Eusebius, *Preparation of the Gospel*, 9.17-18.

[51] Khorenatsi, *History of the Armenians*, 84.

of his might; therefore they made him king over themselves (Gen. 10:9).[52]

Esau the Adversary

In the midrash *Genesis Rabbah*, it is said Esau, the son of Isaac and brother of Jacob, followed the example of Nimrod as a mighty hunter of mankind (JASH. 27:1-3).[53] Esau despised his godly lineage and inheritance and the associated responsibility to bring forth the godly seed (HEB. 12:16). This seed was to be the provider of the *eternal garment of salvation* (ISA. 52:1 61:9-11; JOB 29:14). According to the book of Jasher, and again, the midrash *Pirkei DeRabbi Eliezer*, Esau was jealous of Nimrod because he was in possession of the garments of skin God gave to Adam which gave him his power (GEN. 3:21).

> *Rabbi Meir said: Esau, the brother of Jacob, saw the coats of Nimrod, and in his heart he coveted them, and he slew him, and took them from him. Whence (do we know) that they were desirable in his sight? Because it is said, "And Rebecca took the precious raiment of Esau, her elder son" (Gen. 27:15). When he put them on he also became, by means of them, a mighty hero, as it is said, "And Esau was a cunning hunter" (Gen. 25:27).[54]*

He possessed no faith in the salvific promises of God which the garments only pointed towards. He wanted power and righteousness by his own means. Esau tracked Nimrod in the field as a piece of game and decapitated him to steal the garments from him and consume his power (JASH. 27:3-10). In effect, he abandoned his allegiance to God and his seed, and waved the flag of Satan by stealing the symbolic garment of salvation like the sons of Ham. From here the story connects to the Genesis account of Esau

---

[52] Pirkei DeRabbi Eliezer 24.4.

[53] Genesis Rabbah 37:1-3.

[54] Pirkei DeRabbi Eliezer 24.12.

coming home from the field and selling his birth right to Jacob (Jash. 27:11-13; Gen. 25:29-34). This event was the point in which the godly and ungodly seeds truly diverged and their respective destinies were sealed. Jasher provides an additional layer of potential context for why Esau came home weary and worried that he was about to die. He despised his birth right, the inheritance of the seed, and sold it to Jacob for a single meal, saying "what is this birth right to me?" According to Jasher, it was because he feared vengeance from Nimrod's soldiers and considered himself dead. I think he may have considered the promises of God to be futile now that he possessed the garments which gave Nimrod, the one he so envied, so much power. If Nimrod could ascend in power and mount an offensive against the Most High, what was stopping Esau? In this act he was demonstrating his desire to triumph over the promised seed and claim authority over him.[55]

Divergence of Jacob and Esau

It is clear from scripture that this divergence in the character of Jacob and Esau began in the womb of their mother Rebekah (Gen. 25:19-28; Rom. 9:11-13). The two sons struggled against each other in her womb, foreshadowing the enmity that would exist between them and their peoples:

> *"The Lord said to her, two nations are in your womb, two peoples shall be separated from your body; one people shall be stronger than the other, and the older shall serve the younger" (Gen. 25:23 NKJV).*

These two nations were Israel from Jacob and Edom from Esau. The people of God devoted to spiritual reality, and the people of

---

[55] The Nimrod and Esau connection can be explored in the midrash "Legends of the Jews" by Louis Ginzberg; the journal article "In Search of Nimrod: Nimrod and Esau as Parallel Figures" by Geula Twersky in Hakirah 24, (2018): 215-229; and the website articles "Esau killed Nimrod And Then Sold The Birthright" by Michael Didier, https://weareisrael.org/2014/08/19/esau-killed-nimrod/ and "Facing Longstanding Foes" by Rabbi Fischer https://www.myjewishlearning.com/article/facing-long-standing-foes/.

Satan dedicated to material reality. God said to the serpent in the garden of Eden that between his seed and the seed of the woman, there could never be reconciliation (GEN. 3:15). The lineage of the respective seeds both converge at Isaac. The older son in Esau aligned to the seed of the serpent shall serve the younger in Jacob aligned to the seed of the woman. The seed of the woman shall crush the head of the serpent under his foot.

This divergence was solidified when Esau willingly rejected the counsel and wishes of his parents through his marriage to the two Canaanite women (GEN. 26:34-35; 36:1-4). In his defiance, he set himself apart not to serve God, but to oppose God within the ungodly line. Jacob in contrast went back to Abraham's people to find a wife. The blessing granted to Jacob by his parents for this act of faith further annoyed Esau, who responded by courting a wife from among the Ishmaelites. While Jacob became the father of the twelve tribes, Esau fathered the Edomites and Amalekites with his Canaanite wives (GEN. 36:1-12; 1 CHR. 1:13). His son Eliphaz bore him a grandson named Amalek who became the founder of the Amalekites (GEN. 36:12). The lineage of the Amalekites was thus traceable to the Canaanites (1 CHR. 1:13), and later, other descendants of the sons of Ham, particularly the Philistines (Casluhites) and Caphtorites from the sons of Mizraim (1 CHR. 1:11-12). In a few places in scripture the Canaanites and Amalekites are said to have dwelt together and banded against the Israelites (NUM. 14:25, 41-45; DEUT. 1:42-45). The Book of Psalms records how the Edomites, Amalekites, Philistines of Tyre (Phoenicia), and Assyria, among other groups, formed a confederacy of nations with the goal of wiping out Israel (PSA. 83:1-7). The connection between the Philistines and Caphtorites of Mizraim to the Phoenicians is stressed again by Jeremiah:

> *Because of the day that is coming to destroy all the Philistines, to eliminate from Tyre and Sidon every surviving ally; for the Lord is going to destroy the Philistines, the remnant of the coastland of Caphtor (Jer. 47:4 NASB).*

In a recent study shared by the top academic journal, *Science*, the geneticist Marc Haber discovered that the inhabitants of Lebanon, modern-day Phoenicia, shared 90% of their genes with the sequenced genomes of five 3,700-year-old Canaanite skeletons.[56]

These ungodly peoples actively conspired against God and his holy nation and attempted to thwart His plan for a kingdom of priests (PSA. 83:3-4). Even still, God was less forgiving of the Amalekites, who were supposed to be set apart from the gentiles before God. They were descendants of the Jewish patriarchs Abraham and Isaac, and brothers to the third patriarch in Jacob (later named Israel). Despite their bond, they remained in direct opposition to the descendants of Jacob (Israel) and worked to "prevent the realization of God's plan through Israel" (EXOD. 17:14-16).[57] By doing so, they became the archetypal enemies of the Jews (the sons of Judah-Jacob), and a national representation of the ungodly adversary in Lucifer. The enmity God promised would always exist between the two seed lines from the garden of Eden is represented in this everlasting conflict between Israel and Edom-Amalek.

Israel Tormented by the Descendants of Esau

First, the Amalekites refused safe passage for the Israelites after they came through the Red Sea (NUM. 20:14-21; 21:1-3). They attacked the stragglers at the rear of the congregation as they walked through the wilderness and fought them relentlessly once they entered the land (DEUT. 25:17-19; EXOD. 17:8-16; 2 CHR. 28:17; 1 SAM. 15:1-9; 30:1-4). Edom took revenge on Judah during the destruction of Jerusalem at the hands of Babylon by assisting in its plundering (EZEK. 25:12; PSA. 137:7). The Most High declared that the transgressions of Edom and Amalek will never be forgotten and promises to utterly blot out their names (DEUT. 25:17-19; NUM. 24:14-20;

---

[56] Wade, "Ancient DNA reveals fate of the mysterious Canaanites," Science, https://www.sciencemag.org/news/2017/07/ancient-dna-reveals-fate-mysterious-canaanites.

[57] Diprose, *Israel and the Church*, 17-18.

EXOD. 17:16; OBAD.; EZEK. 25:12-14; 35:5-7; ISA. 34; LAM. 4:21). **Edom, who** presently soars like the eagle and nests among the stars, will be brought down by the Lord and made small among the nations (OBAD. 1:1-9). On the day of the Lord, it shall be done to Edom as they had done to Israel. Jacob will possess his inheritance in the kingdom of the Lord, while Esau will be destroyed (OBAD. 1:8-21).

The spirit of Esau is consistent with the spirit of Antichrist, who like the Edomites and Amalekites, will soon come out from the shadows in an attempt to cripple the people of God. The enmity between the brothers Jacob and Esau, and of their respective peoples of Israel and Amalek, parallels the enmity between the seed of the woman and of the serpent (GEN. 3:15; 25:19-34). They represent the national body of the godly and ungodly lines which stand against each other until the close of the present age, biblically called, this present evil age (GAL. 1:4).

> *"Was not Esau Jacob's brother?" declares the Lord. "Yet I have loved Jacob, but Esau I have hated, and I have turned his hill country into a wasteland and left his inheritance to the desert jackals." Edom may say, "Though we have been crushed, we will rebuild the ruins." But this is what the Lord Almighty says: "They may build, but I will demolish. They will be called the Wicked Land, a people always under the wrath of the Lord. You will see it with your own eyes and say, 'Great is the Lord—even beyond the borders of Israel!' (Mal. 1:3-5 NIV).*

Image 2.2 – Gematria breakdown of Jacob and Esau courtesy of Dafei Tang in the article "Toldot – Secrets of the Twins" for The Times of Israel.

ESAU	JACOB	VALUE
Man of the field אִישׁ שָׂדֶה	Blameless man אִישׁ תָּם	**1371** (620 + 751)
Goat for Azazel הַשָּׂעִיר לַעֲזָאזֵל	Goat for Yahweh הַשָּׂעִיר לַיהוָה	**1371** (730 + 641)

Esau is described as a man of the field and Jacob as a plain (blameless) man living in tents (GEN. 25:27). This gematria breakdown by Dafei Tang relates the two brothers to the two goats used for the Day of Atonement ceremony, the holiest day of the Jewish year (LEV. 16). The goat for Azazel is led into the wilderness in parallel to Esau, the "man of the field," and the goat sacrificed for Yahweh (God) is brought into the Holy of Holies, in parallel of Jacob, the "plain man, living in tents." I believe the presentation of Jesus and Barabbas before Pilate at his sentencing is prefigured by this Day of Atonement ceremony (MATT. 27:15-26; MARK 15:6-15; LUKE 23:13-25; JOHN 18:39-40). This perspective will be discussed in depth in the companion book "Seed of God: Jesus Christ." What we can take from this is that there is an open choice for mankind between the seed of the woman and the seed of the serpent, embodied by the seed of Jacob or Esau; the man Jesus or Barabbas; the Christ or the Antichrist.

Conclusion

Cain, the first man after Adam, set the precedent for fallen mankind in his conduct and godlessness, and in conflict with his brother Abel, outlined the spiritual battleground that has been fought ever since between the godly and ungodly. Following the flood judgement on mankind to destroy the wicked Nephilim on earth, human life in the new world quickly reverted to a comfortable state of sin. It appears the Nephilim which were destroyed in the flood were preserved by one of the wives on the ark, and the ungodly genetics were inherited by the cursed sons of Ham. The new world was doomed to an unregenerate state which required another divine intervention. The ungodly descendants of these sons continue to antagonise the holy people to this day and will do so until the final judgement of God.

3

Preparation for Delusion

The preparation for delusion in its ultimate manifestation over mankind has been millennia in the making. It has found its greatest expression through the kingdoms that have, as it were, been the fountain head of the Babylonian or ancient mystery system. First it was headquartered in Babel, then Egypt and Phoenicia or Canaan, before it was transplanted into the empire of Babylon under Nebuchadnezzar. It was to Babylon where the Jews were deported for seventy-years in judgement because they yielded to the Babylonian mindset and repeatedly violated the sabbatical-year sign of the Mosaic covenant (Lev. 25:2–5; 26:34–35, 43; 2 Chr. 36:21; Dan. 9:2). God made sure that the land could finally lay fallow in the sabbath year so the poor and the animals could find food, and so that the land could recover (Exod. 23:10-11). But the ultimate purpose of their deportation to Babylon was for God to express His will through the source kingdoms of His adversary, Lucifer. God placed a special group of Jews from the tribe of Judah and its royal family within the palace of the king, including the great prophet Daniel (Dan. 1:3-6). Daniel was used by God to reveal the future to the end of the age and the destiny of Israel and the gentiles. More so than any other prophet. The eschatological revelations of Daniel will form the basis of our studies for this chapter. I hope it will help you understand how these prophecies relate to the seed of the serpent to come in the end days.

The Great Statue

The late preacher and bible expositor Derek Prince rightly noted that while Satan's kingdom promises evolution upward to Godhood, in actuality, it is ever devolving downwards to judgement and damnation within the pit of destruction.[58] The great statue that Nebuchadnezzar, king of Babylon, witnessed in a dream testified to this reality (DAN. 2; REV. 12:7-12). As we continue, we will connect the prophetic context of this dream to additional visions from Daniel 7 and Revelation 12-13. Through the description of this mighty statue, we can view history from Babylon to the end of the present age. We will follow the descent through a number of gentile kingdoms known for their terrible influence and authoritarian control over Israel and end with one final kingdom chosen for the seed of the serpent. This kingdom will encompass all the adversarial attributes the previous kingdoms possessed in relation to Israel, and more.

Nebuchadnezzar's Vision

To start off Daniel 2 we read that King Nebuchadnezzar suffered from troubling dreams which troubled his spirit. He sought desperately to understand the meaning and summoned the wise men of the kingdom to provide the interpretation. No one was capable of revealing its truth which God had concealed so Nebuchadnezzar angrily issued a decree to kill all of the supposed wise men of the kingdom. Once Daniel was located and about to be killed, Daniel requested that he be given the opportunity to understand the dream. Daniel received the secret revelation from God in a night vision and hurried to share its meaning with the king and spare the lives of the wise men. These dreams not only related to the reign of Nebuchadnezzar, but the trajectory of the entire world until the end of the age (DAN. 2:24-49). Nebuchadnezzar witnessed a great statue in the shape of a man with a head of gold, chests and arms of silver, belly and thighs of bronze, legs of iron,

---

[58] Derek Prince, "Will The Antichrist Arise In Europe?" June 12, 2015, video, 1:43:20, https://youtu.be/OvKQWvDRiaA.

and feet partly of iron and partly of clay (DAN. 2:31-33). What started from the top as glorious gold devolved into a mixture of iron and miry clay as it reached the bottom.

Daniel's Interpretation

In his interpretation, Daniel identified Nebuchadnezzar as the head of gold and envisioned an inferior kingdom to rise after him which matched the chests and arms of silver (DAN. 2:39). This came to be identified as the Medes and Persians who conquered Babylon during the lifetime of Daniel (DAN. 5:26-31; 8:20). He continued that "a third kingdom, one of bronze, will rule over the whole earth" (DAN. 2:39). This of course matches the belly and thighs of bronze to the incredible exploits of Alexander the Great and the Greeks who defeated the Medo-Persians and most of the known world (DAN. 8:20-21; 10:20-11:14; 1 MAC. 1:1-7). The fourth kingdom, Daniel stated, was to be "strong as iron—for iron breaks and smashes everything—and as iron breaks things to pieces, so it will crush and break all the others" (DAN. 2:40). The enormous empire of Alexander the Great was divided between four of his generals after his death, as prophesied by Daniel (DAN. 11:2-4), and later crushed by the Romans, who were in turn, represented by the legs of iron and feet of iron and clay (DAN. 2:40-43). The imagery of a kingdom that crushes all its opposition by its immense strength characterises the Romans perfectly. The Roman Empire controlled the territories covered by these previous kingdoms. As for the two legs, these are symbolic of the eventual split into the Western and Eastern Roman Empires. Daniel said that the feet and toes of an iron and clay mixture represented a kingdom divided—partly strong and partly weak with "some of the strength of iron in it" (DAN. 2:41-42). This seems to be indicative of this period of weakness or fragmentation of the Roman Empire, or perhaps, of its reconstitution. The next portion of the dream supports the view of a reconstituted Roman Empire. In the dream, Nebuchadnezzar witnessed a rock cut not from human hands strike the statue on its feet of iron and clay and smash them, followed by the rest of the statue crumbling into pieces (DAN. 2:34-35). This suggests that the fourth and final kingdom will have ten toes or be comprised of ten nations or regions, and will be supernaturally defeated by the power of God. Each part is said to be swept away without a trace "like chaff on a threshing floor" and the rock becomes a huge mountain that fills the whole earth (DAN. 2:35). The vision does not seem to line up with the Roman Empire of the past, the more appropriate fit is the final gentile empire which Jesus is to crush on his second coming. Daniel interpreted this vision in this same way, seeing it as a prophetic representation of the end days. He saw a time in which the human kingdoms, ultimately represented by the statue, are completely crushed:

> *In the time of those kings, the God of heaven will set up a kingdom that will never be destroyed, nor will it be left to another people. It will crush all those kingdoms and bring them to an end, but it will itself endure forever. This is the meaning of the vision of the rock cut out of a mountain, but not by human hands—a rock that broke the iron, the bronze, the clay, the silver and the gold to pieces (Dan. 2:44-45 NIV).*

The eternal kingdom of heaven to be set up by God is of course, under the authority of Jesus Christ, the King of kings and Lord of lords (REV. 19:16; 1 TIM. 6:15; MATT. 28:18). He is the rock not of human hands that reduces the human kingdoms to chaff at his second coming of judgement (DAN. 2:31-35; LUKE 20:17-18; ISA. 41:14-15). Jesus identified himself as the stone which although rejected, became the cornerstone upon which the kingdom of God, his Church, is founded (LUKE 20:17). As with Daniel's vision, Jesus warned that in the final days "everyone who falls on that stone will be broken to pieces; anyone on whom it falls will be crushed" (LUKE 20:18).

> *"Listen to me, you who pursue righteousness and who seek the Lord: look to the rock from which you were cut*

> *and to the quarry from which you were hewn" (Isa. 51:1 NIV).*

For all peoples who side with him in that day, he will make Jerusalem a heavy stone or rock which cannot be cut in pieces, "though all nations of the earth are gathered against it" (Zᴇᴄʜ. 12:3). He will enable Israel to finally overcome their oppressors and together they will "thresh the mountains [kingdoms] and crush them, and reduce the hills to chaff" (Isᴀ. 41:14-15). This is in line with Nebuchadnezzar's dream where the mountain he saw acted as a metaphor for a kingdom. The connection between mountain and kingdom is attested to in many places in the Bible (Jᴇʀ. 51:25; Zᴇᴄʜ. 4:7; Rᴇᴠ. 17:9). After the triumphant victory over the Antichrist and his aligned forces, the time of the human kingdoms will be concluded. The greater spiritual kingdom or mountain with Jesus Christ as its king will reign over heaven and earth for ever and ever (Rᴇᴠ. 11:15; 17:14; Jᴏʜɴ 18:36; 1 Cᴏʀ. 15:50).

Interpretations for the Mingling of Men in the Final Kingdom

Daniel said that the final gentile kingdom will be made up of partly strong and partly broken or weak members—they will not naturally adhere to one another. He continued: "they will mingle with the seed of men; but they will not adhere to one another, just as iron does not mix with clay" (Dᴀɴ. 2:43). There are three interpretations of this passage that I am aware of:

1. Intermarriage of the civil and religious powers
2. Intermarriage of the ruling elite
3. Intermixing of the angels and humans as the days of Noah

In regard to the first interpretation, though intermarriage between these powers is clearly happening, I discard it as the main interpretation because in the Bible, *seed* is always related to sexual union or procreation. It could perhaps be partially linked to the goal of integration between Christianity and Islam into the neutered ecumenical religion known as Chrislam.

For the second interpretation, intermarriage between the ruling elite has been commonplace throughout human history to maintain control over resources, major corporations, and royal dynasties. It is clearly still going on—for example, the Rothschild's marrying into the elite Venetian bloodlines of Italy. The elite rulers indeed love to keep control in house, in the family, and they have always done so.

Now for the third interpretation, the intermixing of angels and humans. In the passage of Daniel in question, it is said, "they will mingle with the seed of men; but they will not adhere to one another" (DAN. 2:43). We could interpret "men" as the category of humanity or mankind, and by contrast, "they" as that which falls outside of this category—the alien or angelic. In this view, the mingling is between a supernatural source not of human origin with mankind. As it was in the days of Noah, the offspring of these forbidden unions would show how angels and humans do not "adhere to one another" (DAN. 2:43). Considering Jesus as the ultimate witness to the descent of the fallen angels to Mount Hermon in the days of Noah, and his declaration that the final act of history will replicate the days of Noah, we must give this option serious consideration (MATT. 24:37-39). As mentioned, Jesus quite deliberately led his disciples to Caesarea Philippi at the foot of Mount Hermon to confront Satan and the principalities of darkness (MATT 16:13-18).[59]

I will leave you to consider the three options and decide for yourself what fits best with all the facts presented throughout this book. It is my view that we will witness a combination of the three, with the third becoming the dominant feature at the end.

---

[59] Carpenter, "Why Did Jesus Go to Caesarea Philippi?" *A Carpenter's View*, https://teachingforsotzambia.com/2019/02/20/1040/; Besides what I have wrote in the mentioned place in Chapter Two, I implore you to read "Corrupting the Image" by Douglas Hamp to learn about this angelic corruption of humanity in greater detail.

Ten Toes from Rome

The ten toes of iron and clay come forth from the two iron legs, symbolic of the two divisions of the old Roman Empire that put Rome in control of the Western Empire, and Constantinople (present-day Istanbul, Turkey) over the Eastern Empire. I believe that characteristics of these two closely related empires are expressed symbolically in the feet and toes. We must ask ourselves whether the ten toes arise out of the area of the former Roman East and West divide. It is my belief that there must be a continuation in some significant way.

One possibility is that it describes the European Union, the modern heartland of the Old Roman Empire. In this scenario, the European Union would have ten districts overseen by ten rulers or overseers. Currently the UN has a five-region division with sub regions within each. The nature of this division could always change in the future as the union expands territorially and grows in power. All you have to do is consult a map of Europe before and after the two World Wars to see how quickly and drastically the geopolitical makeup of Europe can change. Such a reality is not considered politically unviable in the current political sphere. The precedent was set all the way back in 1973 when an elite-backed think-tank aptly called the *Club of Rome* explored the prospects of a one world union divided into ten regions (ten toes).

What could possibly follow from this geopolitical shakeup is the reconstitution of the Old Roman Empire. If the divided parties across Europe, the Middle East, and North Africa were reconciled, it would represent the Roman Empire at least symbolically, if not more. These were the areas controlled by the Roman Empire at its height. The precedent for reconciliation has already been set. As early as 1990, five EU member states and five Arab countries set up an initiative called the Western Mediterranean Forum, or the 5+5 Dialogue for these ends. The involved countries were France, Italy, Portugal, Spain and Malta from the EU and Algeria, Libya, Mauritania, Morocco and Tunisia from the Arab world. These kinds of initiatives could be an early glimpse of the necessary consolidation of powers within the European and Arab world for the fulfilment of the final ten toe division of the Roman Empire. This could also lead to the consolidation of the major religions Christianity and Islam, and I imagine Judaism would be included. Combining the three Abrahamic monotheistic religions into one. Ultimately, all we can do is patiently observe the world and the events to come before the true interpretation is realised. Many times the apostles only understood a prophecy once it had been fulfilled, and it will most likely be the same for us.

The Four Beasts

In another apocalyptic vision, Daniel beheld four great beasts emerging from out of the great sea, each with distinct characteristics (DAN. 7). In Hebraic thought, the sea often represents foreign nations or peoples independent of God, called the gentiles (PSA. 65:7; 66:6; 144:7; ISA. 17:12; 57:20; 60:5; JER. 46:7-8; 47:1-2; 51:55-56; EZEK. 26:3). For example, recall the parting of the Red Sea during the exodus from Egypt, in which the Hebrew people crossed on dry ground while the gentile pursuers drowned (EXOD. 14). John of Patmos reinforced this imagery by calling the waters the "peoples, multitudes, nations, and tongues" on which the great harlot sits (REV. 17:1, 15). The rough waters of the sea speak to the chaos and disorder the gentiles are under due to their relationship with the great harlot (ungodly deceptions) and separation from God. The great sea mentioned in this vision doubles as a reference to the Mediterranean Sea which seems to indicate this to be the area from which these beasts emerge, or the capital location of their power.

In the interpretation Daniel receives, the four beasts are further contextualised as being "four kings that will rise from the earth" (DAN. 7:17). In congruence with the vision of the great statue (DAN. 2), the mountain (church of Christ) is clearly described here as "the holy people of the Most High" who are to defeat these gentile kingdoms which fill the whole earth, and go on to possess it forever and ever (DAN. 7:17-18).

As we proceed, it is necessary that we consider two different interpretations of this prophecy in order to establish if there are implications for the future. It will be my own contention that a double fulfilment of this prophecy is a more suitable interpretation. Whichever interpretation is correct, what we can be sure of is that the rock (Jesus) which destroys the great statue (DAN. 2:34) is paralleled by the son of man in the vision of the four beasts (DAN. 7:9-14) who is likewise identified in scripture as Jesus. In the end days, the son of man who is the cornerstone of the Church (mountain) descends on the clouds of heaven to rightfully take back the authority over all nations and all peoples (DAN. 7:13-14; REV 19:11-16). His mountain will indeed fill the whole world (DAN. 2:34-35).

Interpreting the Beasts as the Great Statue

The first interpretation is that the four beasts perfectly mirror the four kingdoms in the dream of the great statue (DAN. 2). These four beasts would thus symbolize Babylon, Medo-Persia, Greece, and Rome. The fact that chapters two to seven of Daniel were written using the poetic structure of a chiasmus would seem to strengthen this connection. The chiastic structure (ABCCBA) is reflected by the identical themes explored in the outer chapters of two and seven (four kingdoms replaced by a fifth), then for three and six (thrown in furnace or den of lions), and four and five (dream interpretations).

In other words, the two visions of the great statue (DAN. 2) and the four beasts (DAN. 7) are relaying the same information but from different perspectives. For Nebuchadnezzar, a great earthly king, the vision of these kingdoms manifested in an inanimate statue which flattered himself. As opposed to Daniel, a great man of God, the same kingdoms manifested as the wild and ferocious beasts totally divorced from the goodness of God. The same reality was portrayed from two perspectives: the earthly and ungodly, concerned with the stature and grandeur of the mortal empires;

and the spiritual and godly, concerned with the terrifying barbarity and wickedness of those who fight in opposition to God.

In this light, the two visions combine to present the history and future of the gentile kingdoms in opposition to the salvation of Israel. Jesus called this period "the time of the Gentiles" (LUKE 21:2). These past historical kingdoms are Babylon, Medo-Persia, Greece, and Rome, and the close of the age will produce a final and most fearsome gentile kingdom. Further dimensions of this kingdom will be unpacked as we proceed in the chapter.

1. The First Beast, the Lion (Babylon)

> *The first was like a lion, and had eagle's wings. I watched till its wings were plucked off; and it was lifted up from the earth and made to stand on two feet like a man, and a man's heart was given to it (Dan. 7:4 NKJV).*

The first beast, the lion, is most certainly referring to Babylon, the head of gold from the great statue (DAN. 2:32, 37-38). Jeremiah described the Babylonian Empire as the lion who devoured Israel, in reference to the conquest and subjugation of Judah during the seventy-year exile (JER. 2:15; 4:7; 5:6; 50:17) The Babylonian Empire was emblematically represented by the winged lion, which denoted the fierceness and swiftness in which it came to authority. In the animal kingdom, the lion and the eagle are of equivalent stature to the head of gold of Nebuchadnezzar. In their comprehensive commentary of the Old Testament, Keil and Delitzsch noted, "what the gold is among metals and the head among the members of the body, that the lion is among beasts and the eagle among birds."[60]

The plucking off of the wings accounts for the destruction of the empire at the hands of Medo-Persia, the second beast. Being made to stand on their own two feet like a man could reflect how,

---

[60] Keil and Delitzsch, "Biblical Commentary on the Old Testament," on Dan. 7:4.

being reduced to ruins, the Babylonians riding high were humbled and made to be like all other lowly kingdoms and peoples.

2. The Second Beast, the Bear (Medo-Persia)

> *And suddenly another beast, a second, like a bear. It was raised up on one side, and had three ribs in its mouth between its teeth. And they said thus to it: 'Arise, devour much flesh!' (Dan. 7:5 NKJV).*

The second beast, the bear, is analogous to the breast and arms of silver in the great statue, therefore representing Medo-Persia (DAN. 2:32). This identification was attested to in the related vision from Daniel 8 of the two-horned ram and the goat, specifically mentioning Medo-Persia as the kingdom which destroyed all that came before it (DAN. 8:3-4, 20). The bear is "raised up on one side" to signify the dominance of the Persians over the Medes. The three ribs in its mouth denote the ruthlessness in which the bear consumed three empires to gain absolute control—Egypt, Lydia and Babylon. Its devouring of much flesh similarly refers to its barbaric hunger for dominance over the nations in its path. This clearly matches the Medo-Persian Empire which, at its peak, ruled over almost half of the world's population.

3. The Third Beast, the Leopard (Greece)

> *After this I looked, and there was another, like a leopard, which had on its back four wings of a bird. The beast also had four heads, and dominion was given to it (Dan. 7:6 NKJV).*

The third beast, the leopard, is represented by Greece under Alexander the Great which battered the Medo-Persian kingdom into submission and overcame the rest of the known world with the blistering speed of a leopard. The same vision from Daniel 8 which identified Medo-Persia as the two-horned ram and the bear mentioned Greece as the goat and thus, the leopard (DAN. 8:1-7, 19-21). The four heads of the leopard are equivalent to the four horns of the related vision, which are explicitly called the four kingdoms which indeed emerged from the kingdom of Alexander after his death (DAN. 8:8, 21-22; 11:2-4).

4. The Fourth Beast, the Most Dreadful (Rome)

> *"After this I saw in the night visions, and behold, a fourth beast, dreadful and terrible, exceedingly strong. It had huge iron teeth; it was devouring, breaking in pieces, and trampling the residue with its feet. It was different from all the beasts that were before it, and it had ten horns. I was considering the horns, and there was another horn, a little one, coming up among them, before whom three of the first horns were plucked out by the roots. And there, in this horn, were eyes like the eyes of a man, and a mouth speaking pompous words (Dan. 7:7-8 NKJV).*

The fourth beast, one not likened to an animal, but the most dreadful and powerful, was Rome. It was Rome that truly shattered the kingdoms that came before it and established an enduring order over much of the known world. Although strong as iron, stamping out all opposition over its long reign, it eventually fragmented and split into the Western and Eastern Roman Empires, represented by the two legs of iron on the great statue. After centuries of this arrangement, their power and influence continued to wane over time until all that remained was consumed by new and more powerful empires. It was never totally wiped out though, and it appears it will be revived in the coming ten nation confederation as shown by the ten horns and by the ten toes from Daniel 2.

The Little Horn

Daniel witnessed a more imposing little horn rise among the ten horns of the fourth beast and *pluck up* three of them (DAN. 7:7-8, 20). In the interpretation of the dream, the ten horns are identified as ten kings from the fourth beast kingdom, and the little horn as another king to succeed them which indeed subdues three kings or horns (DAN. 7:24).

The question is whether these ten horns speak of a past fulfilment or one that is to come. Here Daniel seems to talk of events that have not yet happened and mentions the times, time, and half a time of the abomination of desolation to come at the end (DAN. 7:23-28). This links to John's witness in the book of Revelation which focuses on the same time period, the times, time and half a time, which is just a Hebrew way of saying forty-two months or 1260 days (REV. 12:6, 14; 13:5). Clearly this has not had its fullest manifestation, and a reconstituted Roman Empire might be what it takes for this to be finally fulfilled at the conclusion of this present age.

Image 3.1 – The four parallel empires shown in the visions of the four beasts and the Great Statue.

BEAST (DAN. 7)	STATUE (DAN. 2)	EMPIRE
Lion with wings of an eagle	Head of gold	Babylon
Bear with three ribs in its mouth	Chest and arms of silver	Medo-Persia
Leopard with four wings and four heads	Belly and thighs of bronze	Greece
Beast with iron teeth and ten horns	Legs of iron; feet and toes of iron and clay	Rome

Interpreting the Beasts as Modern Manifestations

The difficulty in interpreting this prophecy comes when Daniel sees the little horn slain and destroyed, but the three beasts are allowed to live without their authority for a period (DAN. 7:11-12). If they are to outlast the final king, the Antichrist, and the False Prophet (REV. 19:20), it would seem that the past kingdoms of

Babylon, Medo-Persia, and Greece are to be ruled out, having long since fallen. If it is indeed true that this vision relates to the kingdoms of the great statue, perhaps aspects of these kingdoms, such as culture and identity, geography, or exploits against God's people are embodied in these future kingdoms? Or at the most extreme end, that these kingdoms are reconstituted?

In the book of Revelation, the little horn and false prophet are said to be destroyed and cast into the lake of fire, but the remaining earthly empires are given time before the ultimate judgement (REV. 19). Could this be a picture of the three beasts from Daniel that are said to outlast the little horn? (DAN. 7:11-12). This quandary leads us into the second interpretation, in which there is a double fulfilment yet future. In this view, the second fulfilment relates the first three beasts to modern empires, with the fourth conglomeration as the beast still to come. This view fits together well with the beast described in Revelation 13, which we shall soon discuss.

Image 3.2 – Potential modern manifestations of the first three beasts.

BEAST	NATION	CHARACTERISTIC	ASSOCIATION
Lion	Great Britain	Eagle wings	United States of America
Bear	Russia	Three ribs	Major conquests
Leopard	Germany	Four heads; four wings	Four Reich's or post-WWII allied division; France

Each of these powers have exerted significant influence over the Jewish people and were instrumental in the reformation of the nation of Israel made possible by the enormous ramifications of World War Two.

1. Great Britain, the Lion

In this interpretation, the lion is symbolic of the British Empire with England as its seat of power. Like the past fulfilment where the winged lion was an emblematic symbol for the Babylonian

Empire, the same is true for England, which, although lacking wings, has been portrayed by the lion since the twelfth century. The strength and stature of the first beast and the head of gold matches well with the British Empire whose territory reached further than any other empire in history, and at its height was called "the empire on which the sun never sets." These days it has since greatly declined in influence and power—or it at least appears that way.

The financial district in London dubbed "The City," still oversees much of the financial destiny of the world. Within its small boundaries are many of the most significant financial institutions of the world and secret-society headquarters. The City is practically a state within a state and does not come under normal English law—it is a sovereign entity in itself, having its own laws, flag, police force, and mayor. Its ruling authority stays hidden, only revealing itself through occult symbols.

The capital of the United States of America, Washington D.C., is a federal district not a part of any state. It functions somewhat independently from the country as with The City in London. It too, is covered with occult symbolism that betrays its so-called Christian foundation.[61] It happens to be that the wings of an eagle seen on the lion speak of the United States of America, whose national bird is the bald eagle, and whose language, financial system, religion, and form of government have its foundations in England. The aforementioned phrase used to describe the global power of the British Empire has been adapted to describe the American power since the twentieth century. While this is certainly the case, it is not fair to call it a complete transfer of power. The two nations have remained deeply intertwined even after the American war for independence from Britain, with persistently strong socio-cultural ties between the peoples and diplomatic standing between governments. They are in a sense, an

---

[61] The Vatican also functions on the same lines as The City of London and Washington DC. It is a sovereign entity separate from Italy and is also plastered in occult symbols.

extension of each other. The United States of today is the leading military power in the world by an order of magnitude, providing the military might behind the dual partnership.

Britain held the mandate for Palestine after World War One and promised the Jewish people their own state alongside a Palestinian State. However, the British reneged on the area promised to Israel, and the Palestinians rejected the two-state solution. The Palestinians have failed to acquire their own independent state to this day. The Middle East problem appears to be a deliberately contrived situation, as further evidence shall show. Israel's return as an independent nation state is part of God's last days redemptive plan, but clearly the counterfeiter has specific designs for this land and its people. He might be trying to pre-empt God's purposes to gain a specific ascendancy, one that I believe will become apparent as we continue.[62]

2. Russia, the Bear

The barbaric and ravenous bear fits the history of Russia which has had no scruples about trampling underfoot all before it—no matter the cost. The three ribs in the mouth of the bear could correspond to the three major Russian victories over the last few centuries. The following is an excerpt from the journal article by Stephen Kotkin for *Foreign Affairs* entitled *Russia's Perpetual Geopolitics*:

> *"History records three fleeting moments of remarkable Russian ascendancy: Peter the Great's victory over Charles XII and a declining Sweden in the early 1700s, which implanted Russian power on the Baltic Sea and in*

---

[62] To better understand the power of this partnership and their roles in the last two World Wars read the following books from Anthony Sutton, "Wall Street and the Bolshevik Revolution," "Wall Street and the Rise of Adolf Hitler," and "The Best Enemy Money Can Buy." Also consider the books "None Dare Call it Conspiracy" by Gary Allen and "The Anglo- American Establishment and Tragedy and Hope" by Carroll Quigley. For viewing, watch "Brotherhood of Darkness and Forbidden Secrets" by Dr Stanley Monteith.

> *Europe; Alexander I's victory over a wildly overstretched Napoleon in the second decade of the nineteenth century, which brought Russia to Paris as an arbiter of great-power affairs; and Stalin's victory over the maniacal gambler Adolf Hitler in the 1940s, which gained Russia Berlin, a satellite empire in Eastern Europe, and a central role shaping the global post-war order.*"[63]

Another scenario is that these three conquests are yet future, and are associated with the preparatory wars in scripture that must precede the battle of Armageddon.

Under Putin, Russia is reasserting itself once again on the world stage and demands to be taken seriously. He is currently exerting a lot of unwelcome influence in the Baltic states and only three continental European countries have called for a response of military force if a NATO member from Eastern Europe was attacked by Russia.[64] Putin will not allow his country to be relegated to the side-lines for much longer. He is very aware that the time to rejuvenate his nation is now or never considering its descending birth rate, declining immigration, and ascending death rate to alcohol abuse and suicide. As of October 2020, the population declined over 350,000 for the year alone, and government projections between 2020 and 2024 estimate a further decrease of 1.2 million people.[65]

Russian governments have historically exercised total control over its people and continue to do so today. The KGB are feared

---

[63] Kotkin, "Russia's Perpetual Geopolitics," *Foreign Affairs* 95, no. 3 (2016): 2-9, https://www.jstor.org/stable/43946851.

[64] Stradner and Frost, "NATO Has a New Weak Link for Russia to Exploit," *Foreign Policy,* https://foreignpolicy.com/2020/04/22/north-macedonia-nato-russia/.

[65] Tickle, "Russian Population to Fall by 1.2 Million by 2024," *RT,* https://www.rt.com/russia/503730-russia-population-estimate-dropping/; To learn about declining population demographics in the first world and how only America is currently bucking the trend, consider reading "America Alone" by Mark Steyn.

for their blatant and ruthless stamping out of all dissent, and of undermining other nations by clandestine means—especially through disinformation campaigns. While communism, one of its greatest exports, seems to have suffered a major blow, this ideology seems to be growing in acceptance in places around the world. The brutal consequences of pursuing this form of governance having long since been established, it is nevertheless becoming more attractive for some because of socio-economic uncertainties and loss of meaning in modern societies. Perhaps the final beast kingdom in the end days will utilise a communist system for its subjects to be wholly dependent on it for subsistence? The mark of the beast would not only be advantageous, but necessary for survival in such a society.

Relevant to the common subjugation of the Jews by these gentile kingdoms, Russia has heavily persecuted its Jewish population over their long and chequered history together. Millions of Jews were kept in systemic poverty for hundreds of years under the Pale of Settlement, a region in which the Jews were confined and shut out from Russian society. Even worse, regular anti-Jewish pogroms swept across Russia in waves over the nineteenth and twentieth centuries, as the Jews were used as a scapegoat for all the ills of society. Unfortunately, much of this stemmed from Christian hatred of the Jews, but the same was true for the secularist communist Russia. The state ideology sought to eradicate religiosity, and the Jews were the most extreme group in which to target and persecute. This treatment persisted throughout the twentieth century, in which they were used as cannon-fodder in the World Wars. The Soviet authorities downplayed and censored the Soviet-Jewish genocide in the Holocaust even after their pivotal assistance on the frontlines. The persistent persecution the Jews suffered in Russia galvanised them to return to Israel and establish their own independent nation. Ever since that time, many millions of Jews have departed from the iron grip of gentile Russia and returned to their homeland.

3. Germany, the Leopard

The leopard beast with the four wings and four heads could be related to Germany (DAN. 7:6). Germany embodied the swift and devastating conquering spirit of the parallel beast empire of Greece under Alexander the Great. Both empires rapidly expanded their territories immediately after consolidating their peoples into a unified whole. In the case of Alexander, this was the formation of a Greek Empire out of the divergent kingdom of Macedonia and the warring Greek city states. Germany had a similar story when in the late nineteenth century Otto von Bismarck masterminded the unification of the many Germanic states within ten years. As a collective, Germany quickly grew into one of the most powerful nations in Europe. Adolf Hitler reinvigorated the crushed German Empire following WWI and managed to devastate Europe and Africa in WWII with blistering speed using the innovative blitzkrieg tactic of warfare.

The four heads of the leopard imply kingdoms, as the metaphor of the head is used elsewhere in scripture as a parallel in the same way as mountains are (REV. 17:9). In the context of Germany, this could potentially refer to a fourth Reich (realms or empires) yet to come. The third Reich of course was the most debased and ghastly empire the world has ever seen, Nazi Germany.

Another possibility is that the subsequent division of Germany into four areas after WWII indicated the death knell of this leopard beast. The four major players of the Allied forces who assumed control of these quadrants just so happen to be the modern nations I believe are referenced in the four beasts. These are England and America (first beast), Russia (second beast), and France (third beast), which is associated with the four wings of a bird on the leopard beast. France has been identified with the Gallic rooster since at least the Middle Ages, which matches the bird of the beast. The European Union is seated in Strasbourg, France, which aligns with the vision of Daniel in which dominion was given unto this beast. As geographic neighbours, diplomatic relations between Germany and France have been paramount, and considering land does not move very quickly, will remain as such. Today, and into the future, the relationship between these two nations is of crucial importance within the European Union. In April of 2020, President Macron of France called for a Weimar triangle of Germany, France, and Poland to help revitalise the European Union dream.[66] Both nations are expected to wield great power on the world stage on behalf of Europe.

In terms of persecution of the Jewish people, it goes without saying that Nazi Germany was the most heinous and formidable threat against the existence of the chosen people. Indeed, Satan's greatest attempt to eradicate the Jewish people and undermine the promises of God to these people was under Adolf Hitler. The identification and numbering systems employed in Nazi Germany to mark the Jews out for persecution and death is an aspect that will be imported into the fourth beast kingdom to come. It is a portent of the future for when the false prophet ushers in the identification system of the mark of the Beast with similar goals (REV. 13:15-18). The silver-lining, if that can even be said, is that the aftermath of the Jewish genocide in the Holocaust was what rallied the world powers to finally re-establish the nation of Israel. A parallel to this is the establishment of the Kingdom of Israel under her Messiah after the final attempt to eradicate this people in the near future.

Germans, along with other European ancestral groups, can trace their culture back to Phoenicia, the old thorn in the back of the Israelites. The god *Esus* derives from the Phoenician god *Isoos* who was based on *Esau*, the Edomite, and the source of Amalek. Esus evolved into the Germanic idol *Odin*, whose warrior shamanism was considered the personification of Germany, especially so for the Nazis. I believe Odin is the clearest picture of the god of forces to be utilised by the Antichrist (DAN. 11:38-39). He

---

[66] Brzozowski, "Macron Seeks Revival of Weimar Triangle," *EURACTIV*, https://www.euractiv.com/section/future-eu/news/macron-seeks-revival-of-weimar-triangle-defence-ties-during-warsaw-visit/.

is characterised by his twisted hunger for war and destruction at all costs.[67]

4. Roman Empire, the Fourth Beast

The fourth beast appears to be a combination of the three that came before but far surpasses them in power and fury. That was certainly true of the Roman Empire which incorporated elements of its predecessors to carve out its own identity. The divergent aspects of these cultures were largely tolerated in order to maintain order and unity within such an expansive and diverse empire. The late Derek Prince made the interesting observation that the belly and thighs of brass representing Greece signified the area of the reproductive organs.[68] Following down from here are of course the legs and feet represented by Rome. This serves as an apt metaphor for a culture that has been reproduced in the western world more than any other. The development of the west owed much to Greek innovation and ideas on governance, religion and philosophy, warfare, architecture, literature, and art. This influence can be seen no more visibly than in the Roman Empire, which by consuming the Greek Empire, inherited their cultural, religious, and political knowledge.

First looking back to the past fulfilment, the territories occupied by the beast kingdoms of Babylon, Medo-Persia, and

---

[67] To learn more about the connection between Germany and Phoenicia there are a number of starting points I will leave you with. I believe the eighth king, the Antichrist will be Phoenician in origin and spiritual inclination, so any connection is significant. The book "Germany and Edom" by Yair Davidy. The articles "DNA Sequencing Traces Ancient Phoenician to Rare European Ancestral Group" by GenomeWeb,
https://www.genomeweb.com/sequencing/dna-sequencing-traces-ancient-phoenician-rare-european-ancestral-group. "Esau Have I Hated!" from Albores, http://albores.net/csp/esau_1.htm. "The Gnostic Nazi" by Moe at Gnostic Warrior, https://gnosticwarrior.com/nazi-gnosticism.html. "Did Ancient Semites Father the Germanic Languages?" by David W. Tollen, https://pintsofhistory.com/2015/01/09/did-ancient-semites-father-the-germanic-languages/. "Odin" by Norse-Mythology, https://norse-mythology.org/gods-and-creatures/the-aesir-gods-and-goddesses/odin/.

[68] Prince, "Will The Antichrist Arise In Europe?"
https://youtu.be/OvKQWvDRiaA.

Greece were all controlled at once by the Romans. In accordance with the dream interpretation, it was "different from all the other kingdoms" by encompassing all the territories of its predecessors (DAN. 7:7, 23). Looking to the future fulfilment, the fourth beast kingdom which is given authority to rule (DAN. 7:6) is said to differ from its predecessors in the sense that it will devour and control the *whole* earth, implying that the previous three never attained total *global* dominance (DAN. 7:23). In an increasingly interconnected and globalised world, it will leverage itself to a dominating position by becoming all things to all people.

John and Daniel as Shared Witnesses

The beast from Revelation 13 and 17 is another component of this image. The deep connection between the books of Daniel and Revelation is well established. The similarities in symbolism between both books are not surprising in light of the fact the heavenly scroll sealed by Daniel to be opened at the end of days is opened in Revelation (DAN. 8:26; 12:4-9; REV. 5; 10:1-7). The scroll in Daniel pertained to the Antiochene persecution to come and is positioned in the context of the abomination of desolations from Antiochus, and finally, the Antichrist. Daniel is told the great persecution of the holy people under the Antichrist "will be for a time, times and half a time" (DAN. 7:25; 12:7) as attested to in Revelation (REV. 12:14). He does not yet understand the vision because "the words are rolled up and sealed until the time of the end" (DAN. 12:9). In other words, the events described in the heavenly scroll are ultimately fulfilled in the time of the Antichrist, and it is Jesus alone who removes the seven seals. The scroll is read one last time in the time of this greater Antiochene persecution before all ungodliness is destroyed with the final judgement.

Beast from the Sea

Similar to the visions of Nebuchadnezzar and Daniel of the great statue and the four beasts respectively, the eschatological visions of John in Revelation are another perspective of the same image:

> *Then I stood on the sand of the sea. And I saw a beast*
> *rising up out of the sea, having seven heads and ten*
> *horns, and on his horns ten crowns, and on his heads a*
> *blasphemous name (Rev. 13:1 NKJV).*

The beast of Revelation 13 and Daniel 7 are both said to have come up from the sea and have ten horns (DAN. 7:7-13). In both visions, the angel explained that the ten horns and crowns speak of ten kings from this fourth beast kingdom (REV. 17:12-14; DAN. 7:23-24). I believe this to be the reconstituted Roman Empire, the ten toes of the great statue (DAN. 2). This fourth beast empire will gain dominance in the not-too-distant future (REV. 13:1; 17:3, 12-14). After these kings, the little horn is said to ascend above them and take control (DAN. 7:8-12, 24-27). This man will be identified as the beast, Antichrist, and the eighth king who persecutes the saints for forty-two months (REV. 11:1-7; 13:3-8; DAN. 7:19-27). In conjunction with this ten-kingdom (or ten districts within the kingdom) authority, the seven heads of this great beast represent the six past kingdoms from Egypt through to Rome, plus re-unified Rome as the seventh. The seven heads of this monster were all animated by the spirit of the occult mystery religious system, Mystery Babylon, who shall for a season exercise enormous influence over the ten kings and for a time—over the beast himself (REV. 17:7, 16-18).

Composite Beast Image

The first three beasts from Daniel—the lion, bear, and leopard—are pictured in the vision of John as the components of a seven headed beast with ten horns and crowns:

> *Now the beast which I saw was like a leopard, his feet*
> *were like the feet of a bear, and his mouth like the mouth*
> *of a lion (Rev. 13:2 NKJV).*

The fourth beast is said to resemble the leopard foremost—as if it is the driving force. Perhaps it means that Germany will become the dominant horn within the reformed ten horn (nation) kingdom. The vision of Daniel agreed with that of John by stating that the leopard beast is given "dominion" or the "authority to rule" (DAN. 7:6). Could these visions be speaking of Adolf Hitler and his Nazi regime, or a future German of Phoenician descent to helm the final hybrid empire?

Moving on, we see that the bear is represented by the feet alone. To me, there is an implication that the Russian force has been limited and may only operate as the feet on the ground, the soldiers. The lion is expressed only by the mouth, which may refer to the dominance of the English language, and the eagle wings appear to have been plucked up in standing with the beast of Daniel. This could indicate that the USA has suffered a sudden decline in power, perhaps lost its superpower status, or has reverted into isolationism.

Conclusion

The Bible gives authority to the testimony of two or more witnesses in order to establish a precedent or judgement (DEUT. 19:15, 2 COR. 13:1). We have discovered there are three separate visions concerning these gentile kingdoms that seek dominance over God's people and land (DAN. 2; 7; REV. 13). No matter what the true representation happens to be, all the lessons learned by the principalities and powers of darkness from all the previous empires will be utilised to the full in the restored Roman Empire, and its final beast king.

4

Catalyst for the Cataclysm

B esides the unholy trinity, there will be one other major player in the last days—"Mystery Babylon the Great, the Mother of Harlots and of the Abominations of the Earth" (JER. 51:1-9; REV. 17:1-7, 16-18). Named as such because she conducts herself like a married woman with many lovers, giving herself over in body and spirit for her own pleasure, self-aggrandisement, and personal gain. Her idolatry is likened to adultery in the eyes of God. In scripture, she is the personification of the mystery religions of the ancient wisdom of Babel, which inherited the occult knowledge of the Nephilim. From the beginning with Babel to the mighty Rome, they all relied on her magicians and sorcerers for guidance and occult insight. They exercised enormous influence over the rulers, who consulted them before making important decisions. For example, Manly P. Hall, one of the greatest authorities on esoteric knowledge, claimed the following about ancient Egypt:

> *"Black magic dictated the state religion and paralyzed the intellectual and spiritual activities of the individual by demanding his complete and unhesitating acquiescence in the dogma formulated by the Priest craft. The Pharaoh became a puppet in the hands of the*

Scarlet Council-a committee of arch-sorcerers elevated to power by the priesthood."[69]

The governments of the current day, in their push for global unity and government, are already acting in the spirit of Mystery Babylon the Great. There is a great effort underway to unite the religions of the world and to dismiss the fundamental and irreconcilable differences present between them. Instead, we are to embrace the commonalities of the many religions and unify around them as one. Those who do not subscribe to this—Christian or otherwise—will be targeted to conform to the objectives of the new order of the age. Human consciousness is currently being shaped according to these Luciferic desires. The convergence towards unity—most significantly through a one world government and religion—is supported by many different efforts intended to acclimate man to the coming Antichrist, the seed of the serpent. To date, a single one world order has come to pass, and that was under Nimrod, who aspired to unseat God from His rightful throne for his own. Another attempt to create a new world order is yet to come with exactly the same objectives. This time it will be executed with absolute confidence by the satanic trinity of Satan, the Antichrist, and the False Prophet, with the help of Mystery Babylon who oversees the spreading of the ancient mysteries throughout the world to divert man away from Jesus, the true Christ. Owing to such efforts, the transformation of human consciousness is in its final stages, and in time, mankind will gladly accept the Ancient Wisdom's saviour as *The Christ*.

One of these great efforts through the centuries is the promotion of the ancient mysteries as the true source of our spiritual heritage. Christianity is framed as a weak counterfeit of this heritage whose existence is damaging to humanity. There is a strong push for this integrated world under the ancient mysteries within the elite political circles in the United Nations, European Union, organisations such as the Council on Foreign Relations

---

[69] Hall, *The Secret Teachings of All Ages,* 101.

(CFR), and the ecumenical religious movement. Many high-profile politicians and leaders from just about every field of endeavour have expressed the need for an international world order for the benefit and survival of planet earth and humanity. The issues of politics, religion, and existential threats such as warfare, financial and ecological collapse, and alien invaders are being manipulated to make this prospect palatable. It may sound good on the surface, but it is incredibly important to understand that this marks the return of the ancient world order under the authority of the former gods of antiquity. If these gods were truly benevolent as some may say, there might be some hope for mankind, but if dominance and control is their real motivation then man has reason to be concerned.

Who is Mystery Babylon?

I believe the end times manifestation of this adulterous woman will be a form of Christianity aligned with a unified world religious system. This blasphemous creation will, in conjunction with the ten-nation confederation, serve to empower the beast (DAN. 2; 7; REV. 13). Throughout history these mystery religions have advanced the plans of Lucifer by misdirecting faith and devotion from the true God. This sets the stage for the seed of the serpent to arrive and be accepted around the world. Lucifer imprinted the symbol of the serpent on the ancient mystery religions to reveal himself as its source. Manly P. Hall pointed out how the serpent was near universally "accepted as the symbol of wisdom or salvation" by the ancient peoples, and claimed, "the serpent is the symbol and prototype of the Universal Saviour, who redeems the worlds by giving creation the knowledge of itself and the realization of good and evil."[70] The Freemasons, to which Hall belonged, are a modern component to this plan with origins in the ancient mysteries. Edmond Ronayne asserted that all the manuals of Freemasonry of the highest authority and merit unanimously agree that "Masonry's ceremonies, symbols and the celebrated

---

[70] Ibid., 88.

legend of Hiram in the Master Mason's degree were directly borrowed from the 'Ancient Mysteries,' meaning the secret worship of Baal, Osiris or Tammuz."[71] So then, the modern custodians of the ancient mysteries take us back to Nimrod, Semiramis and Tammuz—the reincarnation of Nimrod, signifying the continuing relevance of the original new world order. In Ezekiel's vision of the abominations in the God's Temple in Jerusalem, women are seen worshipping Tammuz at the gate of God (EZEK. 8:14). The reference of the gate of God is doubly significant here. The city of Babel in Shinar is called Bab-ilu in the original Babylonian, meaning "gate of God." What Ezekiel saw was a future instantiation of Babylonian worship in the very temple of God, chiefly the Third Temple to be established in the end days.

Perhaps these earthly prototypes derived from the spiritual prototype of Lucifer will again be appropriated to the figures of the times. In addition to Tammuz worship, the Jews were once guilty of worshipping his mother Semiramis, the "Queen of Heaven" (JER. 7:18). Mary, the mother of Jesus, is now called by many the Queen of Heaven. A future pantheon of the gods might match together the prototypical figures of the ancient mysteries to the gods of the world today. In any case, the goal will remain the same—unseat the Most High from His place of authority and establish self-supremacy.

The New Age ecumenical faith is making it possible for Babylon the Great to return to the land of Shinar where she will continue her acts of spiritual adultery without shame or repentance. I believe Zechariah's vision of the woman of wickedness set up in Shinar relates to this great harlot of Mystery Babylon from John's vision (ZECH. 5:5-11; REV. 17:1-18). In Zechariah's vision, the woman in the basket is carried away "to build a temple for her in the land of Shinar" where "she will be set on her own pedestal" once it is prepared (ZECH. 5:9-11). The land of Shinar is Babylon, and the origin point of Mystery Babylon is in the Babylonian city of Babel. I take this to mean she is to be re-

---

[71] Ronayne, *The Master's Carpet*, 7.

established in her first and final place of authority in Babel as per the vision of Ezekiel (EZEK. 8:14). The image of gold which Nebuchadnezzar erected was also on the plains of Shinar. It pointed back to the golden calf statue, the origins of Israelite idolatry, and forward to the image of the beast to one day be established (DAN. 3:1; REV. 13:14-15). Ultimately, they are all the product of the great harlot of Mystery Babylon who promotes the ancient mysteries around the world. Just as all peoples, nations, and languages were forced to worship the gold image or be cast into a fiery furnace (DAN. 3:5-6), the same will be true of worship in the false temple of the Antichrist (REV. 13:8, 14-17). The number of this beast is 666 (REV. 13:18), and the dimensions of Nebuchadnezzar's golden image were sixty cubits high by six cubits wide, and presumably a depth of six cubits due to its omission (DAN. 3:1).

The God of Light

Alice Bailey, the disciple of grand occultist Helena Blavatsky and founder of Lucifer Publishing (renamed Lucis Trust), which exercises great influence at the United Nations, stated directly:

> *"The objective of the new social order of the new politics and new religion, is to bring about the unfoldment of human consciousness ... to bring humanity to the point where it occultly speaking—enters into the light."*[72]

According to Manly P. Hall, this convergence of humanity towards the light is synonymous with "the nobler day when the gods of philosophy once more rule the world."[73] Hall claims they have ruled the world before. In another of his works, Hall claimed:

> *"In the remote past Gods walked with men and they chose from among the sons of men the wisest and truest.*

---

[72] Bailey, *Esoteric Psychology*, Vol. 2, 632; Bailey, *Education in the New Age*, 52.
[73] Hall, *Lectures on Ancient Philosophy*, 38.

> *With these speedily ordained and illuminated souls they left the keys of wisdom."*[74]

This illumination or light is associated with the "Gods [who] walked with men." Could this be referring to the sons of god which Enoch claimed had engaged in unnatural union with human women and transmitted forbidden knowledge and skills such as weaponry, enchantments, and astrology? (1 ENO. 6-10, 15, 55). Azazel, the chief of the fallen angels, was said by Enoch to have "taught all unrighteousness on earth and revealed the eternal secrets which were (preserved) in heaven" (1 ENO. 9:6; 13:1-2).

Albert Pike, as Sovereign Pontiff of Universal Freemasonry, issued instructions to the 23 Supreme Councils of the world on July 14, 1889, to enforce upon the highest degrees (30 and above), a Masonic religion based in the "purity of the Luciferan doctrine." As support for this view, Pike asserted the superiority of Lucifer over Adonai (God):

> *"If Lucifer were not god, would Adonai (the God of the Christians) whose deeds prove cruelty, perfidy and hatred of man, barbarism and repulsion for science, would Adonai and His priests, calumniate Him? Yes, Lucifer is god, and unfortunately Adonai is also God, for the eternal law is that there is no light without shade, no beauty without ugliness, no white without black, for the absolute can only exist as two gods ... Thus, the doctrine of Satanism is heresy, and the true and pure philosophical religion is the belief in Lucifer, the equal of Adonai, but Lucifer, god of light and god of good, is struggling for humanity against Adonai, the god of darkness and evil."*

Hall envisioned a new day for Freemasonry "from the insufficiency of theology and the hopelessness of materialism" in

---

[74] Hall, *What the Ancient Wisdom Expects of Its Disciples*, 23.

which men would turn back to the "God of Philosophy" the "new light breaking in the East."[75] Notice the capitalisation of the *God of Philosophy* to signify that this is the deity, the light-bringer (definition of Lucifer) and the reference to the *East* as its location of power. The east is where the garden of Eden was placed (GEN. 2:8) along with its entrance (GEN. 3:24). After the fall, man departed from the garden in this direction and entered the wilderness both spiritually and physically. From the occult perspective, this is not seen from the perspective of shame and guilt but as a sign of liberation. The wilderness under Lucifer was symbolic of freedom from the prison of God. Albert Pike stated, "to all Masons, the North has immediately been the place of darkness, and the great lights of the Lodge, none have been in the North."[76] Robert Ingham Clegg, 33rd Degree Freemason, likewise wrote that "in Freemasonry the North is the place of darkness" and described how Masonic altars contain lights in all directions but the north.[77]

Scripture seems to attest to the idea of heaven, God's dwelling place, as being situated in the North (ISA. 14:13; JOB 26:7; 37:22; PSA. 48:1-2). Burnt offering sacrifices, which were the prefiguration of the salvific sacrifice of Jesus, the lamb of God, were carried out and offered "at the north side of the altar before the Lord" (LEV. 1:1-11). It is said "exaltation comes neither from the east nor from the west nor from the south" (PSA. 75:6). North is the only cardinal direction left unmentioned, which implies the abode of God is to our north. For the Jews, land to the north was considered higher than that of the south. Many verses describe those who travelled from south to north as going up (GEN. 45:25; HOS. 8:9; ACTS 19:1) and those who went from north to south as going down (GEN. 12:10; 26:2; 38:1; 1 SAM. 25:1; 26:2; 30:15-16).[78]

---

[75] Hall, *Lectures on Ancient Philosophy*, 454-455.

[76] Pike, *Morals and Dogma*, 592.

[77] Mackey, "North, Altar, and East," in *Encyclopedia of Freemasonry*.

[78] McClintock and Strong, "North," in *Cyclopedia of Biblical, Theological and Ecclesiastical Literature*, vol. 7, 59.

With this information in mind, consider how Lucifer said: "I will sit also upon the mount of the congregation, the sides of the North" (ISA. 14:13). Lucifer is viewed by these occult figures as the God of Philosophy and the Bearer of Light:

> *"Lucifer the Light Bearer! Strange and mysterious name to give to the Spirit of Darkness! Lucifer the Son of the Morning! It is he who bears the light, and with its splendour's intolerable blinds feeble, sensual or selfish souls."*[79]

Accordingly, Adonai the God of Israel from the North is regarded as the darkness but Lucifer from the East is the true light. They anticipate for Lucifer to extend his light into the North of darkness, the dominion of God, in place of the true light of Jesus. That is to say, he will defeat the Most High and take for himself the authority of the third heaven in the North. The mindset of man is being shaped to accept this new king in the place of the true God. The adherents of the ancient mysteries patiently await the universal return to the ancient wisdom and the ancient gods. Henry Clausen, the 33° Freemason, similarly "looked forward to a transition into a New Age using the insights and wisdom of the ancient mystics."[80]

Modern culture is already saturated with stories of gods, superheroes and aliens through our film and literature. This is not accidental or incidental to the times and seasons we live in. But first, the present and existing world order that is based on a Judeo-Christian worldview must be done away with, as hinted at by Hall on the insufficiency of theology. These so-called "forces of evil" said Bailey, "must disappear if the New Age is to be ushered in as desired."[81] In this New Age culture and civilisation which she envisions, she expects orthodox Christians to "reject the theories

---

[79] Pike, *Morals and Dogma*, 321.

[80] Clausen, *Emergence of the Mystical*, 19.

[81] Bailey, *Esoteric Psychology*, Vol. 2, 630-632.

about The Christ which occultism presents" but the masses will no longer "accept the impossible deity of the feeble Christ which the Christian endorses."[82]

The occultists are working on the premise that by bringing their Christ more favourably into the light, Christians not sufficiently knowledgeable in the Word of God will find it difficult to hold to the biblical revelation of Christ as Lord. Gradually they will yield their place of separation from the world and assume the mindset of unity of all types. Sadly, millions of Christians are being seduced by their messaging, and induced to reject the one who alone is unleavened bread (Hebrew idiom for purity and righteousness), and accept the counterfeit who is all leaven. In their unbelief they are helping millions of unbelievers stay firmly in their unbelief. If there is one sin, one clear definition of missing the mark in Hebraic and Christian thought, it is unbelief. At the heart of unbelief is pride, and the heart of pride is rebellion.

Jewish Misdirection

The basis of the Jewish faith, the Tanakh (OT), has been distorted and superseded by Rabbinic thought, and the pervasive influence of Jewish esoteric mysticism, notably Kabbalah. These aberrations of the ancient mysteries have created enormous hurdles for the Jewish people to understand biblical revelation and how it pertains to their future. Even two-thousand years after their saviour came and died for them, the Jews are still blind to his face (2 COR. 3:14; ROM. 11:25). If the adherents of these systems, such as the Kabbalists, truly understood the foundational teachings of the Tanakh, much less the New Testament, they would realize it is antithetical to biblical teaching. For a people who choose to remain under the Mosaic Law, the sorcery and demonic divination which is practiced in these systems is a grave sin in the eyes of God (LEV. 19:26, 31; 20:6, 27; DEUT. 18:9-12; 2 KGS. 21:6).

The practical dimension of Kabbalah involves rituals for gaining and exercising power to effect change in our world and in

---

[82] Bailey, *The Externalisation of the Hierarchy*, 589-590.

the celestial worlds beyond ours. This power is generated by performing commandments, summoning and controlling angelic and demonic forces, and otherwise tapping into the supernatural energies present in creation:

> *The practical aspect of Kabbalah furthers God's intention in the world, advancing good, subduing evil, healing, and mending. The true master of this art fulfils the human potential to be a co-creator with God.*[83]

Naturally, the esoteric method of Kabbalah in Jewish mysticism lends itself well to Freemasonry, which seeks the counterfeit light. Albert Pike expressed this sentiment in *Morals and Dogma*:

> *Masonry is a search after Light. That search leads us directly back, as you see, to the Kabbala. All truly dogmatic religions have issued from the Kabbala and return to it; everything grand in the religious dreams of the Illuminati, Jacob Boehm, Swedenborg, Saint-Martin, and others, is borrowed from the Kabbala; all the Masonic associations owe to it their secrets and symbols.*[84]

Eliphas Levi, considered the greatest occultist of the nineteenth century, was one among many of his time who related Kabbalah to the occult. According to Rosemary Guiley, author of *The Encyclopedia of Witches, Witchcraft and Wicca,* Levi was one of the non-Jewish occultists responsible for the growing interest in Kabbalah during the nineteenth century.[85] Levi related the Kabbalah to the Tarot and numerology and drew connections to Freemasonry, in which he saw a fusion of Judaic Kabbalism and

---

[83] Dennis, "What Is Kabbalah?" *Reform Judaism,*
https://reformjudaism.org/beliefs-practices/spirituality/what-kabbalah.

[84] Pike, *Morals and Dogma*, 741.

[85] Guiley, "Kabbalah," in *The Encyclopedia of Witches, Witchcraft and Wicca*, 190-91.

Neoplatonic Christianity. The Kabbalah, he said in *The Book of Splendours*, is one of three occult sciences of certitude; the other two are Magic and Hermeticism.

Christian Complicity

The Apostle Paul warned that just before the appearance of the Antichrist there will be an ultimate rejection of God, or *apostasia* in Greek, from which we get the English word apostasy (2 THESS. 2:3). In the last days people will depart from the faith, giving heed to seducing spirits and doctrines of devils (1 TIM. 4:1). Offering worship to God while doing the same for any combination of other gods is no different than rejecting him outright. This is the danger of the ecumenical movement, for the Word of God is the truth, *nothing* about it is relative. A world where truth is no longer a unifying principle of eternal reality, but a *hindrance* to unity, is one where the emergence of the Christ of the mystery religions is possible. The ultimate apostasy occurs in conjunction with God dropping His forceful restraining of evil so that man may see the true consequences of his actions. The ungodly trinity are at last given full reign over their earthly subjects.

Ecumenical Shift

Today there are popular Christian leaders under this ecumenical delusion who undermine the God of Israel and Christianity whom they are supposed to support (EPH. 2:11-22; ROM. 11). Pope Francis is well-known for stressing the commonality between Christianity and Islam to promote a "Human Fraternity" of the Abrahamic religions. Some suspect (myself included) that the end-goal of these efforts are some kind of fusion of Christianity and Islam, or Chrislam. In 2019, the Pope signed a joint statement called the "Document on Human Fraternity" with the Grand Imam Ahmad al-Tayyeb to strengthen the interfaith dialogue. In his own words, "this was no mere diplomatic gesture, but a reflection born of dialogue and common commitment."[86] Indeed, a concrete response to this declaration was quickly realised with the announcement of the Abrahamic Family House that is to be built in Abu Dhabi. Designed to advance the interfaith goals of the treaty, it is to be an interfaith place of worship consisting of a mosque, church, synagogue, and educational center. You must wonder what concessions will be made in the future to appease each of the involved parties. It is hard to imagine negotiations will tip in the favour of Jews and Christians considering how the Islamic shrine, the Dome of the Rock, is atop the Jewish Temple Mount, and the perimeter fence displays the scathing words against Christianity, "God has no son."

Besides the ecumenical focus, Pope Francis has recently called for "fundamental reform and major renewal" of the international economic order and the "development of a form of global governance."[87] In his encyclical letter from 2020, *Fratelli Tutti*, the Pope claimed, "it is essential to devise stronger and more efficiently organized international institutions" (V. 172) and stressed "the need for a reform of the 'United Nations Organization' and likewise of economic institutions and international finance, so that the concept of the family of nations can acquire real teeth" (V. 173). At the papal visit to the United Nations in 2015, Pope Francis put forth important proposals for this reform and renewal of the UN system:

> *Francis insists that the intergovernmental system must develop effective juridical frameworks that can hold governments to account for their "solemn commitments" ... notions of state sovereignty need to change so that the U.N. system can have more power over governments, including through the creation of "instruments of*

---

[86] Pope Francis, *Fratelli Tutti*, sec. 5.
[87] Ibid., sec. 132, 179.

> *verification" to measure, evaluate and regulate commitments.*[88]

With this in mind, the following question stands. Are these efforts towards world governance and religious unity centred in love and truth or the works of the Babylonian ancient mysteries?

Catholic Monuments of Idolatry

It would happen that the Catholic Church has many associations with the Phoenician and Babylonian mystery religions. For example, the Catholic cardinals, bishops, and the Pope all wear a mitre hat which resembles the open mouth of a fish. This was directly adopted from the headgear worn by the priests of Dagon, the Canaanite (Phoenician) fish-god, and the father of Baal. The Bible mentions Dagon several times as a false idol worshipped by the Philistines who stole the ark of the covenant to be housed with their god Dagon (JUDG. 16:23; 1 CHR. 10:10; 1 SAM. 5:1-18).[89]

There is an enormous Roman fountain of a pinecone called *Fontana della Pigna* which stands at the Vatican. The pinecone was considered sacred in Egypt and Rome and was related to the opening of the third eye—the eye of illumination. What was the serpent's goal in the garden if not to open man's eye of illumination and seek independence from God and His sovereign truth?

Another instalment is the ancient Egyptian obelisk situated in its centre of St. Peter's Square in the Vatican City. It was moved to Rome by Caligula in AD 37 and moved to its current location in 1586. The obelisk symbolised the sun god Ra, another beacon of false light (sun). Who instructed them to place these symbols there?

---

[88] Ahern, "Pope Francis Calls for a Stronger System of Global Governance," *America,* https://papalvisit.americamedia.org/2015/09/25/pope-francis-calls-for-a-stronger-system-of-global-governance/.

[89] The fate of Dagon and the Babylonian religion are clearly revealed in the video, "The Capture of the Ark" by Pastor Bill Randles, https://www.youtube.com/watch?v=p8hslXzqagg.

Multitudes believe that a Pope will be the final Antichrist, but it is my firm conviction that the Papacy is instead the domain of the Harlot of Mystery Babylon. Her residence is in the ecumenical, interfaith movement presided over by the Papacy. If the Pope does not become the channel for Mystery Babylon, another religious leader of sufficient stature and charisma will step forward and claim the role in the near future.

Protestant Involvement

We have focused extensively on the Catholic complicity in this ecumenical shift, but do not think that the Protestant world is exempt from similar criticism. Indeed, the many denominations and its most prominent leaders are just as guilty of embracing false idols and false teachings. For example, the former representative of eighty-million Christians in the Anglican church, Rowan Williamson, who was previously the Archbishop of Canterbury, adopted a dual-priesthood of Anglican and Celtic Druid, an ancient pagan faith.[90] The druids were recorded by Julius Caesar, Cicero, Suetonius, Lucan, Tacitus, and Pliny the Elder as being ritual performers of human sacrifice.[91]

The most deceptive and wicked of the Protestant affronts to Christianity is the widely popular modern spectacle of wealth, prosperity, and self-esteem gospel by the likes of Kenneth Copeland and Benny Hinn. In this underworld of Christianity, biblical faith is promoted as a force to be tapped into (for a fee) to accrue wealth and improve your status among men. The unsuccessful and downtrodden are considered to be so simply because they lack faith (or funds) to invest in their perverted prosperity gospel. Such a definition would have eliminated many of the apostles and early believers from the Church. Truthfully, scripture explicitly instructs us to take no other gods before God

---

[90] BBC, "Archbishop Becomes Druid," *BBC News*,
http://news.bbc.co.uk/2/hi/uk_news/wales/2172918.stm.

[91] Lucan, *Pharsalia*, i.450–458; Caesar, *Gallic Wars* 6.16, 17.3–5; Suetonius, *Claudius* 25; Cicero, *Pro Fonteio* 31; Cicero, *On the Republic*, 9.

(Exod. 20:3). The gods of materialism and self-Godhood which infest these televangelist churches are no different to the Baals of the past. Instead, we are called to deny ungodliness and worldly lusts, and live soberly, righteously, and godly (Titus 2:12).

We are also witnessing today the rise of the Christian witch movement which purports to tap into deeper knowledge available through non-traditional religious practices such as sorcery. The first annual conference was held in 2019 at Salem, the location of the famous Salem witch trials. The tool of visualization is employed for ritualistic purposes to manifest images of "spirits and gods, symbols, and other aspects of ritual."[92] The prosperity preachers misuse this same mental imagery technique to mislead and steal from those most in need. It appears the faith of prosperity preachers and the sorcerers work by one and the same spirit. Jesus gives a powerful warning to those who claim to work by his Spirit but are actually empowered by the counterfeit:

> *Many will say to me in that day, Lord, Lord, have we not prophesied in thy name? and in thy name have cast out devils? and in thy name done many wonderful works? And then will I profess unto them, I never knew you: depart from me, ye that work iniquity (Matt. 7:22-25 NKJV).*

While the ecumenical shift is ramping up now, it has been a slow and gradual encroachment on the orthodoxy of the faith. These acts would have been untenable at the time of the first meeting of the Parliament of World Religions in 1887. The Papacy and the counterfeit faiths, including the Protestant denominations which are aligned with Babylon the Great, are all too comfortable upon the back of the beast kingdoms of this world. They are totally oblivious to the reality that *they* are being taken on the ride to destruction along with her (Rev. 14:6-8; 17:1-7, 15-18; 18). Yes, they face a judgement ordained by the God whose truth they refuse to

---

[92] Guiley, "Visualization," in *The Encyclopedia of Witches, Witchcraft and Wicca.*

acknowledge or come to in humility. In an ironic twist, God allows the very Beast whom they have confidently believed to be in control of, to be the means of their own judgement for all the blood they have shed across time (REV. 16:17; 18:5-8; ISA. 47:7-13). All other religions will perish, including the worship of the trinity from Babel of Nimrod, Semiramis and Tammuz, and only one form of worship for man will remain—the worship of the ultimate man of sin, self-exalted above all (DAN. 11:36; 2 THESS. 2:3-4).

World Government

The trend towards religious unification and dilution of biblical truth is a necessary component for the future political unification around the world. These two worlds must merge as one to allow the false light, the Antichrist, to emerge. Major efforts are currently being undertaken to achieve this goal even though outwardly things still seem very fragmented and divided. That fragmentation is being used carefully to create a deeper desire for peace and a hatred for all forms of divisions, so they cry all the more for this elusive state. We shall now seek to outline the current political efforts to achieve this long-term plan as well as ascertain our own placement on this prophetic timeline.

Robert Muller, the former Assistant Secretary-General of the United Nations, began working there near the beginning of its formation and stayed there for forty years. He devoted his entire career to the realization of this reality within the United Nations. In his work *My Testament to the UN* Muller said the following:

> *The UN must be the mother and teacher of the peoples of the world concerned not only with the fullness of their lives, but also with their soul. The UN will become the world's common religion, a universal spirituality.*[93]

In his eyes "peace will be impossible without taming the fundamentalist through a United Religion that professes

---

[93] Muller, *My Testament to the UN*, 171.

faithfulness only to the global spirituality and the health of the planet."[94] Muller claimed that the religions of the world will eventually combine into a united whole under the United Nations. Those which stay out will learn to regret it in the same way nations regretted not joining the UN or EU earlier.[95]

In this same book, Muller quoted Sri Chinmoy, whom he called the "United Nations Guru" to explain "the spiritual journey of the United Nations." Sri Chinmoy claimed that the "United Nations is the vision-light of the Absolute Supreme" who waits for the divine success to be realised, at which time "the Absolute Supreme will ring His own victory bell here on Earth through the loving and serving heart of the United Nations."[96] In light of what we have learned thus far, ponder the identity of the Absolute Supreme who is said to descend to earth and ring his victory bell in the United Nations.

Telling Symbolism from the Elites

Symbols are a deliberate tool employed by the governmental custodians of the ancient mysteries to covertly communicate their purposes. In confidence they display these symbolic messages in plain sight, fearing not the privy few, for they are confident those ignorant will remain as such. Hall had this to say on the importance of symbolism in his book *The Secret Teachings of All Ages*:

> *In a single figure a symbol may both reveal and conceal, for to the wise the subject of the symbol is obvious, while*

---

[94] A remark from Muller to Rev. Swing at the inaugural United Religions Initiative summit of June 1996.

[95] The following report from Robert Muller outlines his hopes for a world government and the birth of a global religion from the ashes of fundamentalism in the same way the UN reduced national fundamentalism he considers to be sovereignty: https://earthcharter.org/wp-content/assets/virtual-library2/images/uploads/Robert%20Muller%201999.pdf.

[96] Muller, *My Testament to the UN*, 172.

> *to the ignorant the figure remains inscrutable. Hence, he*
> *who seeks to unveil the secret doctrine of antiquity must*
> *search for that doctrine not upon the open pages of books*
> *which might fall into the hands of the unworthy but in*
> *the place where it was originally concealed.*[97]

A recent example which can be viewed for yourself is the 2016 Gotthard tunnel opening ceremony in Switzerland. On display for the crowd of European elites, including the leaders of Germany, France, Italy and Switzerland, were blatant occult symbolism.[98] At the end of the ceremony, a goat-man resembling Baphomet is seen mocking a lamb, the symbol of Jesus. The goat robed in white (Pan or Lucifer) dies and is resurrected as a red cloaked woman (the scarlet woman or Semiramis of Rev. 17).

The European Union is also known for openly displaying their reverence of the ancient mystery religions through artwork, sculptures, and architecture. The principal building of the European Parliament, the Louise Weiss building, was built in the image of the famous Pieter Brueghel painting of the unfinished Tower of Babel to openly declare their aspirations of restoring the ungodly stronghold of Bavel or Babilu—the gate of god. This connection was emphasised in an EU poster titled "Europe: Many Tongues, One Voice" in which the tower of Babel is seen undergoing modern renovations from the Europeans to accomplish the aims of its ancient predecessor. Above the tower are twelve stars in the shape of pentagrams (occult symbol of Baphomet), who is the aforementioned goat-man.

Outside various European Union institutions, including the Louise Weiss building, are statues of the Phoenician princess Europa (derived from Astarte, then to Semiramis, mother and wife of Nimrod) atop a white bull (Zeus). Europa is considered the

---

[97] Hall, *The Secret Teachings of All Ages*, 20.

[98] Hume, "World's Longest Tunnel Opens Deep beneath Swiss Alps," *CNN*, https://edition.cnn.com/2016/06/01/europe/switzerland-longest-tunnel-gotthard/index.html.

personification of Europe. This parallels Babylon the Great riding the beast. This is the world religious system, united as one and exercising authority to the point of apparently controlling the beast himself (REV. 17). This bull, or image of the beast, is also in the top-left corner of all European Union residence cards.

Alien Diversion

Over the last one hundred years the alien threat has captivated the imagination of the public. One great incident was the "dancing sun" witnessed by seventy-thousand people at Fatima, Portugal in 1917. UFO researchers claimed this to be a legitimate encounter. This event was linked to an appearance of the "Virgin Mary" who was given the title "Our Lady of Fatima."[99] This worship of Mary is a convenient tool to deceive Christians and acclimatise them to the idea of supernatural alien manifestations from another dimension.

The Search for New Life

The Vatican, the bastion of Catholic Christianity, is itself guilty of Mary worship and complicit in this alien scheme. The Catholic Church has developed one of the largest telescopes in the world at Mount Graham in the United States. The Jesuit astronomers in charge state emphatically that they are searching for alien life and when questioned on what to do should they find it, replied "baptise them into the Church."[100] The Vatican astronomer Giuseppe Tanzella-Nitti suggested that in the event of extra-terrestrial contact, Christians would have to conduct a re-reading of their faith "inclusive of the new data" once the religious content originating from outside the earth had been verified.[101] Thankfully

---

[99] Sumner, "Our Lady of Fatima, UFOs, and September 1994," *Hebrew Streams*, http://www.hebrew-streams.org/works/hayom/fatima-ufo-rapture.pdf.

[100] Jha, "Pope's astronomer says he would baptise an alien if it asked him," *The Guardian*, https://www.theguardian.com/science/2010/sep/17/pope-astronomer-baptise-aliens.

[101] Tanzella-Nitti, "Extraterrestrial life," *Interdisciplinary Documentation on Religion and Science*, 4.2, http://inters.org/extraterrestrial-life.

he does not believe such a discovery would nullify the Christian faith altogether, but what exactly this scientific recalibration would entail is by no means clear.

The theologian Ted Peters noted how the scientific knowledge surrounding astrobiology, or the existence of alien life, is "frequently mixed up with myth."[102] He stated that theologians use the term "ETI myth" to describe how the scientific "assumption of progress within evolution" leads many to hold a quasi-religious belief in the existence of extra-terrestrial intelligent beings (ETI) that are "more advanced than earthlings in evolution and technological progress." These types suggest that "more highly evolved ETI could bring scientific salvation to planet earth" and "save earth from its primitive and under-evolved propensity for violence."[103] Whether or not Tanzella-Nitti had this in mind for the potential scientific recalibration of the faith is not clear, but it is a strong possibility.

If we are being primed for potential contact with an extra-terrestrial and godlike foe, I believe it is less out of curious exploration and more as a tool for fear and domination. The pre-emptive solution to quell the fears of the people would be obvious—prepare for the worst by forming a worldwide governmental system to better deal with the threat. To achieve maximum cohesion and unity, rules for governance and living will be enforced from the top-down.

A Return to the Days of Noah?

Another dimension to the alien phenomena is the theory of interbreeding between the species, similar to the forbidden relationship between the fallen angels and human women. Dr John E. Mack was a former head of Psychiatry at Harvard Medical School, and later became a researcher in the psychology of alien abduction experiences. In his book *Abduction: Human*

---

[102] Peters, "Astrotheology and the ETI Myth," *Theology and Science* 7, no. 1 (2009): 4.

[103] Ibid., 3.

Encounters with Aliens, Mack collated his research and experiences with supposed alien abductees:

> *The pioneering work of Budd Hopkins and David Jacobs has shown what is amply corroborated in my cases, namely that the abduction phenomenon is in some central way involved in a breeding program that results in the creation of alien/human offspring ... My own impression is that we may be witnessing ... an awkward joining of two species, engineered by an intelligence we are unable to fathom.*[104]

Computer scientist and author Jacques Vallee wondered if the two species were cross-bred in order for the aliens to maintain physical contact with us. Under this theory, these entities require a living human medium to materialise into human form.[105] The resemblance to the Nephilim incursion is uncanny. But Vallee, an atheist, goes further by tracing back the origins of these supernatural experiences to the biblical stories of the Nephilim in his book *Dimensions: A Casebook of Alien Contact*:

> *Are these races semi-human, so that in order to maintain contact with us, they need cross breeding with men and women of our planet? Is this the origin of the many tales and legends where genetics play a great role: the symbolism of the virgin in occultism and religion, the fairy tales involving human midwifes and changlings, the sexual overtones of the flying saucers reports, the biblical stories of intermarriage between the Lords angels and terrestrial woman whose offspring were giants?*[106]

---

[104] Mack, *Abduction: Human Encounters with Aliens*, 401-403.

[105] Vallée, *The Invisible College*, 233.

[106] Vallée, *Dimensions: A Casebook of Alien Contact*, 404-405.

These men say the space invaders are messengers and masters of deception who come from another dimension, not part of the natural space-time continuum, and under no circumstances should we make contact with them. However, the transformation of human consciousness which is the centrepiece of the New Age evolution is so far advanced that we now have so-called Christian institutions actively seeking their confidence. The potential of alien-human hybrids, or more correctly, angelic-human hybrids as in the days of Noah, is a very real potential, as per the promise of Jesus (MATT. 24:37-39). The judgement of water destroyed the old world dominated by the Nephilim, but the "present heavens and earth are reserved for fire" (2 PET. 3:2-13). Could this be an indication of a second angelic or alien incursion upon earth with a similar divine judgement to come?

Global Environmental Collapse

Let me preface by emphasising that I am not questioning how issues of sustainability, pollution control, and energy efficiency can be tackled from a place of good intention. Instead I am focusing on the top-down global agenda being propagated that assumes a dangerously authoritarian dimension. I believe that the authority of these global governing bodies will eventually be extended beyond reasonable levels, and those who question this will be treated as heretics. The degraded environmental condition and the need for global solutions makes way for the governments of the world to propose global solutions to avoid catastrophe and restore order. The following is an excerpt from the 1992 Youth Sourcebook by the International Institute of Sustainable Development (IISD) which summarises this perspective:

> *The environment issue was set up as a global issue in need for global action. There were demands to strengthen international law, which could make nations toe the line ... efforts at the global level directly contributed to a sense of global identity, or global citizenship which would be the first step towards global*

> *governance. Such global governance would further distance power from the people while giving unlimited access to governments and multinationals ... The co-operation of NGOs also plays a role in global governance. In order to appear democratic, the illusion of a strong opposition allowed to voice grievances is essential. By selecting and allowing a certain opposition to function, all other opposition is easily painted as radical and extremists.[107]*

Environmental modification techniques (ENMOD) or weapons, have also been developed which can be harnessed for environmental good, but just as easily fall into the hands of bad actors with malicious intent. These sophisticated tools possess the capability to change weather patterns, create natural disasters, and destabilise agricultural and ecological systems. The danger of these tools in military hands is apocalyptic in nature. ENMOD is but another weapon of mass destruction in the arsenal of the world powers. Both the US and Russia are known to possess these capabilities, with China and other antagonistic nations no doubt following behind them.[108]

> *Weather-modification, according to the US Air Force document AF 2025 Final Report, "offers the war fighter a wide range of possible options to defeat or coerce an adversary. Capabilities, it extends to the triggering of floods, hurricanes, droughts and earthquakes. The ability to generate precipitation, fog and storms on earth or to modify space weather ... and the production of*

---

[107] IISD, *Youth Sourcebook on Sustainable Development*, http://iisd.ca/youth/ysbk000.htm.

[108] Chossudovsky, "The Ultimate Weapon of Mass Destruction," *Global Research*, https://www.globalresearch.ca/the-ultimate-weapon-of-mass-destruction-owning-the-weather-for-military-use-2/5306386.

> *artificial weather all are a part of an integrated set of [military] technologies.*"[109]

An existential crisis, manufactured or not, would bring the populace into submission to the global governmental bodies for protection. The surrendering up of autonomy could extend to nations if a global integrated effort between nations was deemed necessary for survival. An expectation or condition could be to relinquish certain sovereign rights to the global institutions for the sake of *security*. Nations that are presently committed to their own national sovereignty must be steered towards a universal mindset before the emergence of this global government.

Technology of the Gods

> *Within thirty years, we will have the technological means to create superhuman intelligence. Shortly after, the human era will be ended.*[110]

The continuing acceleration of technological growth and advancement is launching the world into a future unrecognizable from the past. A world destined to hit a critical point of complexity that scientists call the *singularity*—or more esoterically, the *Omega point*.[111] The Jesuit priest and scientist Teilhard de Chardin posited that God is the moving force behind this evolution, and that all of creation inevitably develops towards a final point of unification called *Christogenesis*. In his view, Christ is both the *cause* and the *purpose* of evolution, as the "Alpha and Omega, the beginning and the end" (REV. 21:6). The Omega point is considered to mark a new level of spiritual consciousness and

---

[109] Ibid.

[110] Vance, "Merely Human? That's So Yesterday," *New York Times*, https://www.nytimes.com/2010/06/13/business/13sing.html.

[111] Essential reading on the topic of the singularity is the book "The Singularity Is Near: When Humans Transcend Biology" by Ray Kurzweil.

religion, and the final manifestation of the *Total Christ.*[112]

> *Will man become a mutating GMO, a humanoid robot, a*
> *hybrid or both? Will his life be extended much longer or*
> *even indefinitely? Will he reproduce in vitro in the near*
> *future? These are questions we should be asking*
> *ourselves now, for our children will likely experience*
> *these changes, but our grandchildren will live in quite a*
> *different world.*[113]

New scientific fields such as astrobiology, robotics, genetic engineering, and artificial intelligence have transformed the way man perceives the world and its future. The idea of superhuman intelligence or major human genetic modification is no longer relegated to science fiction. While researchers disagree about the extent of these technological developments, there is a strong possibility that humans will eventually interface with computers and modify their own biology. Brain-machine interfaces are already being developed by companies such as Neuralink, and the CRISPR gene editing technique has shown enormous potential. Some are far more optimistic about the future, presenting a world where humans are fully integrated with super intelligent machines and are no longer bound by the biological death principle.

As a result of these technological developments, philosophies such as transhumanism have stepped up to advocate for a *posthuman* future and provide a framework for those living in such a reality. Many are putting faith in this idealistic world of self-Godhood where human limitations are greatly surpassed. Now ask yourself, can I imagine how this misdirection of faith away from God and into self-Godhood may align with the purposes of Lucifer? Consider how the serpent assured Eve "you shall not surely die" when death was to be a consequence of eating from the

---

[112] Delio, "Teilhard De Chardin and The Future of God," *Center for Christogenesis,* https://christogenesis.org/teilhard-de-chardin-and-the-future-of-god/.

[113] Fillard, Is Man to Survive Science? Book blurb or description.

tree (GEN. 3:4). Don't you think if man overcame death, he would render God unnecessary as a saviour?[114]

The Death Principle

The Nobel Prize winner Richard Feynman said, "it is one of the most remarkable things that, in all of the biological sciences, there is no clue as to the necessity of death." From the biblical perspective, the clue to the necessity of bodily death is summed up in the words "thou shall not" that incurred the promise, "thou shall surely die," but of course, this verdict is rejected by man. This curse of sin necessitates death. Death is not defeated by increasing sins, but the total absence of sin. We continue to assure ourselves of our own authority over God and strive to escape death altogether despite our inescapable fallen natures. To pass beyond the first death back to life requires a redirection of our faith into the resurrection of Christ. We cannot find salvation anywhere else. As a man, Jesus was absent of all sin, and therefore innocent under this Luciferic covenant. Accordingly, upon his death, death itself was unable to hold him. Because covenants are binding until death, when Jesus died and came back to life, the Luciferic covenant was broken. Now man is free to cut a new covenant with Christ by following him to the cross in faith. Upon death, all in Christ do not remain in the grave, but are raised out of their mortal bodies of corruption and into an immortal and incorruptible one (1 COR. 15:53). Through him we can confidently say: "O death, where is thy sting? O grave where is your victory?" (2 COR. 15:55). The new heaven and earth that is prepared will transcend any human potential that awaits us, which judging by the history of man, will devolve into a dystopic nightmare before the day of judgement.

Nevertheless, the human objective for omnipotence is too tantalizing for us to pass up. According to Yuval Harari in his book, *Homo Deus: A Brief History of Tomorrow*, "omnipotence is in

---

[114] Bostrom, "A History of Transhumanist Thought," *Journal of Evolution and Technology* 14, no. 1 (April 2005): 1-25, https://www.nickbostrom.com/papers/history.pdf.

front of us, almost within our reach ... but below us yawns the abyss of complete nothingness."[115] The columnist Michael Gerson commented on this for the Washington Post, and seemed to think "a humane future will require someone to offer a bridge across the chasm."[116] This very someone is identified biblically as the Antichrist. He will bridge this seemingly impossible chasm by rising from the dead and overcoming the death principle, although the push is on already within the scientific community to achieve this by technological means. People will naturally desire to follow his example, and to attain such abilities, will gladly meet any requirements that he imposes. We can assume these demands to include the redirection of all worship to himself, and to receive his mark for loyalty (REV. 13:16-17). The mark of the beast could very well be a means of accessing this posthuman technology, and those who refuse it would not only lose the ability of buying and selling, but of the tempting posthuman capabilities presented. In a world fully intertwined and connected with technology, to refuse the mark is to essentially sign your own death sentence.

Atheism Hijacked

Just as Christians are targeted to be silenced or compromised, in the proposed glorious New Age, the same is true for the atheist who holds steadfastly to religious unbelief. Unfortunately for them, worship is a Luciferic requirement. There is no place even for atheism in the ungodly line. Even Freemasons acknowledge this and require all prospective Masons to believe in a god. The naturalist philosophy that is popular among atheists has been hijacked by these ungodly forces to cultivate the growing anti-Christian sentiment. The intent is to utilise the movement insofar as it remains useful, as is the case with the mystery religions.

---

[115] Harari, *Homo Deus: A History of Tomorrow*, 201.

[116] Gerson. "Humans reach for godhood," *Washington Post*, https://www.washingtonpost.com/opinions/humans-reach-for-godhood—and-leave-their-humanity-behind/2017/06/26/5f74b20c-5a93-11e7-9fc6-c7ef4bc58d13_story.html.

Naturalism is the idea that the observable world can be fully explained by natural properties and causes in place of supernatural or spiritual explanations. Instead of taking natural science as a means of describing the creation of God, they go one step further and assert that there must be a fundamental contradiction between science and God. Many believers become discouraged in their convictions by this popular argument, and are afraid of simply questioning popular scientific assertions (or dogmas) for the fear of appearing dogmatic or backwards. When clear battle lines are drawn with no grey area in-between, the outcome is apparent—many grow resentful of God the creator or reject Him outright—falling right into Satan's trap.

More Gods to Replace God

In an interview with the leading voice for atheism, Richard Dawkins, interviewer Ben Stein questioned Dawkins on the possibility of intelligent design as working in tandem with naturalist science.[117] Dawkins side-stepped the implication of a divine Creator, but still found himself having to entertain the idea of *panspermia* as a designer for man, the idea that extra-terrestrials are the propagators of life on our planet:

> *Dawkins: "It could be that at some earlier time, somewhere in the universe, a civilization evolved, probably by some kind of Darwinian means, probably to a very high level of technology, and designed a form of life that they seeded onto perhaps this planet ... I suppose it's possible that you might find evidence for that if you look at the details of biochemistry, molecular biology, you might find a signature of some sort of designer."*

He did not mention what could have produced or designed these aliens. Dawkins is not the only naturalist atheist who considers

---

[117] Dawkins, interview by Ben Stein, *Expelled: No Intelligence Allowed*, April 18, 2008. video, 2:01, https://youtu.be/BoncJBrrdQ8.

this viewpoint. In fact, the supernatural appears to be in vogue so long as God is disqualified. Dr. Clay Routledge, a professor of psychology, has written extensively on this subject and sees a strong association between low religiosity and belief in alien incursions on earth. In an article for Psychology Today, he referenced a poll done in the United Kingdom which found "about 42% of UK residents believe in UFOs but only 25% believe in God."[118] He continued that "belief in alien visitors and other fringe magical beliefs such as belief in ghosts seems to be increasing" and in a personal study, found about 7% of atheists completely rejected the existence of UFOs while well over half reported some confidence. The cause in his eyes, and in my own, is that as "countries become less invested in traditional Christian beliefs, they become more interested in non-traditional spiritual practices, ghosts, UFOs, healing crystal, psychic powers, and so on."[119]

The Deadly Manipulation of Atheism

The atheist rejection of the true God naturally leads them towards accepting alternative explanations for the order and design in creation. Without God to lead them in the right direction, that which steps in God's place aligns with the ideals of the Luciferic Age. All the way back to the 1870s, Albert Pike, the Sovereign Grandmaster of Scottish Rite Freemasonry, supposedly wrote the following letter to revolutionary Giuseppe Mazzini highlighting how the Luciferic ideal is to eradicate all religious belief and unbelief that is not directed at Lucifer:

> *We shall unleash the Nihilists and the atheists, and we shall provoke a formidable social cataclysm which in all*

[118] Routledge, "Atheists Love Aliens" *Psychology Today,* https://www.psychologytoday.com/blog/more-mortal/201504/atheists-love-aliens.

[119] Vail, "The Religious Mind is in the Heart," *Psychology Today,* https://www.psychologytoday.com/us/blog/tree-life/201807/clay-routledge-the-religious-mind-is-in-the-heart.

its horror will show clearly to the nations the effect of absolute atheism, origin of savagery and of the most bloody turmoil. Then everywhere, the citizens, obliged to defend themselves against the world minority of revolutionaries, will exterminate those destroyers of civilization, and the multitude, disillusioned with Christianity, whose deistic spirits will from that moment be without compass or direction, anxious for an ideal, but without knowing where to render its adoration, will receive the true light through the universal manifestation of the pure doctrine of Lucifer, brought finally out in the public view. This manifestation will result from the general reactionary movement which will follow the destruction of Christianity and atheism, both conquered and exterminated at the same time."

Alice Bailey described how the eradication of all other religious belief will facilitate the arrival of this God of Light:

"Forget not that our planet is not yet a sacred planet, though it is close to that Great Transformation, when that which overshadows Him during this incarnation has wrought the needed changes through a process of transformation and transmutation then a Great Transfiguration will take place and He will take His place among those empowered to work through a Sacred planet."[120]

Who is this Man who will undergo a Great Transfiguration and establish a Sacred planet? Listen to a statement by his forerunner—his John the Baptist as it were, Benjamin Creme, about the one he calls Maitreya, the Christ:

---

[120] Bailey, "The Fourteen Rules for Group Initiation," in *The Rays and Initiations*, rule 13.

> *"One day soon, men and women all over the world will gather round their radio and television sets to hear and see the Christ: to see His face, and to hear His words dropping silently into their minds - in their own language. In this way they will know that He is truly the Christ, the World Teacher; and in this way, too, we will see repeated, only now on a world scale, the happenings of Pentecost; and in celebration of this event Pentecost will become a major festival of the New World Religion. Also, in this way, the Christ will demonstrate the future ability of the race as a whole to communicate mentally, telepathically, over vast distances and at will."*[121]

Another reference is made to the Tower of Babel, the prototype of the world government in cosmic opposition to God. When the Tower is metaphorically rebuilt, God will not be there to confuse the tongues, the Beast will indeed communicate to all his slaves in their own language. As for the reference to Pentecost, the first Pentecost was inaugurated at Mount Sinai at the giving of the Law by the hand of God, and the second followed the resurrection of Jesus Christ. Here we are told of another Pentecost to come through a different Christ—one who will possess miraculous powers and be hailed as the *World Teacher*. This is the event that will inaugurate the new Aquarian Age and end the Piscean Age— an age considered to represent dogmatism and exclusiveness. All faiths will be required to join the one universal faith or perish. The ecumenical movement, along with the New Age movement and the United Nations, are currently working overtime preparing the world for this universal religion and the appearance of the Christ.[122]

---

[121] Creme, *The Reappearance of the Christ and the Masters of Wisdom*, 29.

[122] To better understand this process of global spiritual integration read, "The Altar" by Ian Wishart.

How God is in Control

This omega point can only unfold under the sovereign oversight of the Most High—who in His wisdom will allow this outworking of the Luciferic agenda because man chooses to love falsehood rather than truth. God always gives us what we want, holding nothing back from us despite the claims of man or the demonic realm. He has sent multiple messengers through the centuries with the call to know and love the truth, but man prefers to stay in darkness (JOHN 3:19). In this environment of apostate belief and religious practice, similar to Israel in the day of Hosea the Prophet (HOS. 8:1-6), God will remove His restraining hand over the evil powers so man can see the inevitable degeneration that occurs without the light of God. Man will reap what he has sown "for they have sown the wind, and they shall reap the whirlwind" and since they "have ploughed wickedness, they shall reap iniquity" (HOS. 8:7). Why? Because they have eaten the fruit of lies (HOS. 10:13). The whirlwind of iniquity they shall reap are the members of the unholy trinity who shall soon appear onto the world stage in full force. To indulge in mind and spirit with Mystery Babylon is to eat the fruit of lies. The acceptance of the False Prophet and Antichrist will be the natural result. The God who declares that He and He alone is the living God will hold man to account for this refusal to love the truth and the acceptance of *The Lie*, which is the ultimate expression of iniquity in the person of the man of sin (2 THESS. 2:3). Here the Greek emphasises the lie as the definite article, *The Lie*. A strong deluding influence will flow over mankind for their unwillingness to receive a love for the truth, and God will see to it that they love the lie and embrace it (2 THESS. 2:9-11). The work of the principalities and powers through occult and pagan influences have been so successful that mankind willingly serves the creature rather than the Creator (ROM. 1:18-32).

The greatest expression of The Lie is at the door. When the omega point is reached, the unfolding spiritual evolution will be such that all will be primed to worship the great master of deception, and he will finally ascend to the throne he most desires—the Davidic Throne belonging to Jesus, the ultimate Davidic king (1 CHR. 17:11-15). He will be a man who reveals himself God above all gods (2 THESS. 2:4, DAN. 11:36-37) and when he assumes total control, he will not just expect, but demand the worship of all—including the atheists (REV. 13:8, 16-17). All will be required to receive either his mark, name or number, to prove their faith in him as God (DAN. 11:36-37; 2 THESS. 2:3-4; REV. 13:7-8).

Conclusion

God has granted Mystery Babylon ample time to repent, but His time of judgement is unmovable. Right before the conclusion of the 490 years spoken of by Daniel, God will execute judgement upon her (JER. 51:6, 47; REV. 14:8; 18:4-10). The merciful God warns all faithful to her to come out from her grasp to avoid such a fate (REV. 18:4-5). No one, not even Christians, are exempted if they indulge in her false teachings.

> *Little children, it is the last hour; and as you have heard that the Antichrist is coming, even now many antichrists have come, by which we know that it is the last hour. They went out from us, but they were not of us; for if they had been of us, they would have continued with us; but they went out that they might be made manifest, that none of them were of us. But you have an anointing from the Holy One, and you know all things. I have not written to you because you do not know the truth, but because you know it, and that no lie is of the truth. Who is a liar but he who denies that Jesus is the Christ? He is antichrist who denies the Father and the Son (1 John 2:18-22 KJV).*

This scripture reveals that the Antichrist spirit works primarily in Christian environments where the truth has been proclaimed and known but not yielded to. Those who are not genuinely of the truth will always move away from it. Therefore abide in Jesus Christ and him alone. Stand among the ecclesia, the called-out ones, to serve within his Church. Place your faith in the testimony of God and

His word. He will shield you from His coming wrath against wickedness. He will defeat the evil forces which deceive and pull us away from Him. Do not allow yourself to be distracted by counterfeits that may have the appearance of the truth but work in deception of the worst kind (GAL. 1:8-9). The deadliest counterfeits are the ones that are so very close to the true pattern.

> *But I am afraid that just as Eve was deceived by the serpent's cunning, your minds may somehow be led astray from your sincere and pure devotion to Christ. For if someone comes to you and preaches a Jesus other than the Jesus we preached, or if you receive a different spirit from the Spirit you received, or a different gospel from the one you accepted, you put up with it easily enough (2 Cor. 11:3-4 NIV).*

Scripture instructs us not to love the world—we are not to give ourselves to the spirit, attitude and mindset of this present evil age (2 COR. 10:3-5). We are to take captive every thought and idea that rises against the knowledge of Jesus and the truth.

> *"Beware lest anyone cheat you through philosophy and empty deceit, according to the tradition of men, according to the basic principles of the world, and not according to Christ. For in Him dwells all the fullness of the Godhead bodily; and you are complete in Him, who is the head of all principality and power" (Col. 2:8-9 NKJV).*

We are to use our critical faculties and the Word of God to help us discern the signs of the times, and not allow our minds to be shaped by the zeitgeist, the spirit of the age. Armed with this attitude we can be equipped by the Holy Spirit to recognise deception and stay separated from it. This will be a necessary component of our lives as we enter the concluding drama of the age and the arrival of the seed of the serpent.

5

The Concluding Drama

I n this book we have journeyed through the serpent line from the initiation at the tree of the knowledge of good and evil in the garden of Eden, down through Cain to Tubal-Cain before the flood, and from the sons of Ham after the flood. We have investigated the gentile kingdoms which these ungodly ancestors have established in opposition to the God of Israel and considered the ultimate manifestation to come in the end days. The focus of this final chapter will be to uncover the ultimate seed of Satan, the Antichrist. For this undertaking, we are to once again consult the prophetic visions of John in the book of Revelation. John sees seven kings and seven gentile kingdoms as being responsible for the manifestation of an eighth king, the Antichrist:

> Then I saw a beast coming up out of the sea, having ten horns and seven heads, and on his horns were ten crowns, and on his heads were blasphemous names (Rev. 13:1 NASB).

The angel provided the following interpretation of the vision for John:

> The beast that you saw was, and is not, and is about to come up out of the abyss and go to destruction ... The seven heads are seven mountains upon which the woman sits, and they are seven kings; five have fallen, one is, the

> *other has not yet come; and when he comes, he must*
> *remain a little while. The beast which was, and is not, is*
> *himself also an eighth and is one of the seven, and he goes*
> *to destruction (Rev. 17:8-11 NASB).*

The first fragment to unpack in the revelation of the beast is the fact that he has been here before, he "was and is not," and is set to return. John saw the beast come up out of the sea, a metaphor for the spiritual wilderness that is the bottomless pit, or the abyss. As we discussed in the third chapter, the sea is a common biblical metaphor for the wilderness of the gentiles, the absence of God. Fittingly, the angel carried John away into a wilderness to explain his vision (Rev. 17:3-8).

Seven Heads as Kingdoms

Next, we have the symbolism of the seven heads that are seven mountains, and of the woman who sits upon them. The most widely accepted view considers the seven mountains to be the hills of Rome, which was known as the city of seven hills. The fact that Rome was the empire in control at the time of John lends credence to this idea. Jerusalem also happens to be a city of seven hills and is the city the gentile kingdoms desire most. The view I am partial to however, and which fits in with my understanding of the subsequent passages, is that the seven heads or mountains are seven kingdoms, and the woman is Mystery Babylon, the womanly personification of the mystery religions. The connection between mountains and kingdoms is well established. In other words, these six kingdoms were subject to the prevailing influence of the mystery religions and exercised their power accordingly by persecuting the Jews (Luke 21:24; Rom. 11:25). The seventh and final kingdom will inherit this adversarial position towards God and His people and increase the persecution to its limit. The previous kingdoms will find their expression in the seventh through the shared subservience to the woman, and consequently, their opposition to Israel and the promised son of their faith. There is much scripture that supports this final seventh kingdom being a reformation of the previous sixth kingdom, that of iron, but in a weakened form of iron mixed with clay (DAN. 2; 7; REV. 12:3; 13:1).

The dreadful beast, the eighth king and Antichrist, is seen with ten horns and ten crowns (DAN 7:7-8; REV. 13:1-10). These ten horns, or ten toes from the great statue (DAN. 2), are identified by the angel as ten kings who serve the beast in the seventh kingdom (REV. 17:12-13). We learnt in Daniel 7 that from these ten horns or kings the little horn, or beast king, is to spring up and subdue three of the kings (DAN. 7:23-25). Under his authority, these horns will rule with the beast for a short time (REV. 17:12-13). With these findings in mind from the third chapter, a reformed Roman empire is the clear candidate for the seventh kingdom and the Antichrist is the eighth king (DAN. 2; 7; REV. 13). He will be the embodiment of all the ungodly characteristics of these kingdoms and its kings.

Image 5.1 – The seven potential kingdoms or heads from Revelation 17.

SEVEN KINGDOMS – PAST (5) PRESENT (1) FUTURE (1)	
1. Egypt	*Past kingdoms*
2. Assyria/Phoenicia	*Note: Babel was the first human kingdom under Nimrod, but Egypt was the first from the establishment of the Israelite people. This was the first gentile empire that exerted itself against the chosen people of God.*
3. Babylon	
4. Medo-Persia	
5. Greece	
6. Rome	*Present kingdom (at time of John)*
7. Reconstituted Rome (unknown)	*Future kingdom*

Some interpreters conclude that the beast that was, now is not, but then is, refers to the restoration of the Roman empire after centuries in which it was not. If the empire were reconstituted, this could potentially align with the healing of the deadly head wound prophecy (REV. 13:3, 12-14). Such an accomplishment would be hailed as a successful resurrection from the dead. However, the beast is said to ascend out of the bottomless pit (abyss), which is a holding place for beings, not kingdoms (REV. 11:7; 17:8). The text explicitly states that the seven heads *also* refer to seven kings, of which five were from the past according to John, one in the present (Rome), and one yet to come. This distinction indicates that the seven heads are simultaneously kingdoms *and* kings—the two are intertwined. John seems to reinforce this literal interpretation of the seven kings by telling us the beast (who is not an entity, but a man) is the eighth king, and is of the seven. John uses the pronoun *he* and *him* when mentioning the beast (Rev. 13:3-8), as does Daniel (Dan. 7:24-25; 8:11-12; 12:36-39).

Who is the Eighth King?

The question then is what does it mean for the eighth king to be of the seven? The first possibility is that the eighth king is "of the seven" in likeness and nature. That is to say, he will be the perfect embodiment of the previous ungodly kings in their opposition to God and His people. In this sense, the prophecy of John would enable us to identify the Antichrist via the recapitulated acts of his predecessors.

The second possibility is that the eighth king is literally one of the seven kings from the past—he was, is not, yet will be. In this situation he will experience a second-coming alongside Jesus Christ. The question that follows is which of the seven kings was the first incarnation of the Antichrist? John stated that it would take a mind of wisdom to discover the answer. If the eighth king is simply the seventh king, where is the wisdom in discovering that? By this I mean, if a future king arises and through a death and resurrection experience transforms into the eighth king, what purpose was there in asking the people in John's day (first century AD) to exercise the mind of wisdom to identify the eighth king? How could they possibly know who the eighth king was? What purpose would the previous kings serve? There are a number of possibilities to consider here. There is still the possibility that the seventh king is yet to come, and the duty of identifying him will fall on future believers, or possibly ourselves. The seventh king is said to reign for only "a short space" (Rev. 17:10). Perhaps this refers to the three-and-a-half years the beast (Antichrist) rules before he suffers the deadly head wound and resurrects? Or perhaps the eighth king will claim to be the reincarnation of one of the first six kings, like how Saddam Hussein claimed he was the reincarnation of King Nebuchadnezzar? In any case, when he is resurrected from the dead the whole world will marvel and follow him (REV. 13:3-4).

My own contention is that to identify the eighth king before he appears, not after, is the mark of wisdom which the angel told John. This requires us to ponder and ponder again to identify this man correctly. The answer might be found from among the five who had fallen before John's day (late 90AD) because to John the beast "was and is not." That is to say the beast had fallen or died. But we are told that the beast is to be revived and "come up out of the abyss," the bottomless pit (REV. 11:7; 17:8).

The abyss (bottomless pit) is known to be the holding place of the rebellious angels who violated God's principle of separation with man (REV. 9; JUDE 6-7; 1 PET. 3:18-20; 2 PET. 2:4-7; 2 ENO. 18-3). It is mentioned nine times, which is symbolic of finality and judgement, and is said to have a king rule over it called *Abaddon* in Hebrew ("a destructive one or place of destruction"), and *Apollyon* ("destroyer") in Greek (REV. 9:1-2, 11). Is he Azazel, the leader of the company of angels who descended to Mount Hermon in the days of Noah, and is now held in the abyss? The Azazel goat portrayed by Barabbas in opposition to Jesus during his trial? (MATT. 27:15-17). I liken Abaddon or Apollyon to the fourth beast which was and is not, who will ascend out of the bottomless pit and become united with the eighth king, the Antichrist before its time of destruction (REV 17:8; 13:1-10; 11:7). The vision of the dreadful beast, the Antichrist, who rises from the sea (REV. 13:1-10) is explained by the angel as ascending from the abyss, or the bottomless pit (REV. 17:8). This stands in contrast to Jesus Christ, who said he is, "who is and who was and who is to come," when he descends from above to come and destroy the beast and save the saints (REV. 1:8; 6:12-17; 11:15-19; 19:11-21; MATT. 24:29-31).

Requirements of the Eighth King, the Antichrist

I encourage you to refer to the attached biblical references for the following characteristics of the Antichrist. These scriptures inform us on the requirements to look for out of the eighth king, the Antichrist. Firstly, he will be a ruler of Phoenician origin from the Great Sea, the Mediterranean Sea (EZEK. 28:2, 12-15; ISA. 10:12; DAN. 7:3). The reference to the Great Sea could also indicate his origin in gentile humanity in opposition to the God of Israel. He will ascend within a reunified ten nation empire (DAN. 7:24) with the support of a small base (DAN. 11:23). He, the Assyrian (identified by Ezekiel as Antichrist figure), will be like a cedar of Lebanon—a man who stands taller than all others in stature and prowess (EZEK. 31:3). His great intelligence and awareness of political matters will be utilised to deceive and flatter his way to the top (DAN. 11:21). In fact, he will be wiser than all men to have lived, and no secret will be hidden from him (EZEK. 28:3). A leader of Israel, the False Prophet (REV. 13-11-18; ZECH. 11:15) possibly from the tribe of Dan, will assist his ascendancy, bringing the fulfilled return of Rome from the sea with its ultimate Caesar.[123] Supremacy over the kingdom will come peaceably through deceptive modes of intrigue and flattery (DAN. 11:21-24). This new Caesar will further the peaceful facade by facilitating a peace treaty between Israel and the surrounding nations for seven years (DAN. 9:27; 11:24).[124] He will then shoot above the ten rulers as his plans gain acceptance within Israel and the world (EZEK. 31:5). Three of these ten rulers will challenge his position but will be removed from their place of authority (DAN. 7:8, 20). He will seek to bring world peace in order to give the appearance of a messianic age befitting a Messiah of the Light. He may promise to militarily protect Israel if she will yield her army to his control in exchange for peace. He could then grant the

---

[123] Sanhedrin 21b.

[124] What is rather fascinating about this seven-year covenant is that seven to year interim peace deals have been proposed in former peace talks between the Israeli's and the Palestinians. These temporary peace deals would serve as a buffer period before a further permanent and binding agreement.

Israelites the right to rebuild the Temple in Jerusalem, next to the Dome of the Rock, and also bring the Christian witness in Jerusalem under this Abrahamic umbrella, establishing Jerusalem as a place of prayer for all nations. He would receive immediate honour and status for helping to conclude this into an effective and binding peace. Therefore, when the Israel-Palestine issue and the need for a two-state solution is once again brought centre stage in international affairs, the eighth king, the Antichrist, will be a voice that begins to be heard with calls for a new Temple in Jerusalem as a necessity to bring peace and unity.

Masonic Connection

Undoubtedly, in the modern context he will need strong connections in Europe and the Middle East, and hold links to the United Nations. He will likely be a Freemason steeped in the ancient mysteries, and be part of, or in favour of the ecumenical movement—at least until he is able to supersede it. This man will be enthusiastically supported by three very important organisations clearly identified by master occultist Alice Bailey:

> *The Masonic Movement ... will meet the need of those who can, and should, wield power. It is the custodian of the law; it is the home of the Mysteries and the seat of initiation. It holds in its symbolism the ritual of Deity, and the way of salvation is pictorially preserved in its work. The methods of Deity are demonstrated in its Temples and under the All-seeing Eye the work can go forward. It is a far more occult organisation than can be realised and is intended to be the training school for the coming advanced occultists ... in Masonry you have the three paths leading to initiation. As yet they are not used, and one of the things that will eventuate — when the new universal religion has sway and the nature of esotericism is understood — will be the utilization of the banded esoteric organism, the Masonic organism and the*

> *Church organism as initiating centres. These three groups converge as their inner sanctuaries are approached. There is no dissociation between the One Universal Church, the sacred inner Lodge of all true Masons, and the inner-most circles of the esoteric societies.*[125]

Here we are told of the importance of Freemasonry and its link to apostate religious networks (ecumenism) and secret esoteric societies. Bailey emphasises that the groups will converge in worship of one Universal God in One Universal Church, the Temple. It will be "the sacred inner Lodge of all true Masons, and the inner-most circles of the esoteric societies." To facilitate the Antichrist's rise to everlasting power, these custodians of the ancient mysteries under Mystery Babylon have gone to endless lengths to set the necessary conditions for the Jewish people to return to the land of Israel and begin rebuilding the Temple at Mount Moriah. With their God of Light (Antichrist) seated in the Temple, they will be unified in his worship and wield power over mankind for a short period of time. The building of a Third Temple in the exact image of the former Temples will be trivial:

> *It is known to every reader of the Bible and student of Solomon's days, that an amazingly detailed description of the Temple and its associated structures has been carried down from the mists of antiquity by the Scriptures. Lineal measurements, materials employed, and ornamental detail are so graphically presented that restoration of the Temple, at any time within a score of centuries past, awaited only the coming of a man with the vision to recognize its historic value, and the imagination to undertake the task."*[126]

---

[125] Bailey, *Externalisation of the Hierarchy*, 511, 513.

[126] Kelchner, *The Bible and King Solomon's Temple in Masonry*, foreword.

Great efforts have already made available all the necessary furniture, utensils and priestly vestments for service in such a rebuilt Temple. A red heifer required for the ritual purification required to start Temple worship and sacrifice is apparently ready.[127] The unfolding of these current events indicate that the eighth king's ascension from the abyss may be in the not-so-distant future.[128]

After the Temple has been established, the Antichrist will evolve into Godlike status when he overcomes his own death from a fatal head wound (REV. 13:3, 12-14). The whole world will marvel at his triumph over the death principle and accept his self-declaration as God (DAN. 11:37-38; 2 THESS. 2:3-4). With the world's support, he will be emboldened to commit the abomination of desolation by sitting in the Most Holy Place of the Temple and proclaiming himself as God (2 THESS. 2:4; REV. 13:14). The setting up of his image in the Temple by the False Prophet will set in motion the Great Tribulation spoken of by Daniel and Jesus (DAN. 12:1; MATT. 24:21). The False Prophet will exercise his authority to inaugurate the final act of worship of the one he lifts up in honour, with the introduction of the requirement for all to receive either the mark, name, or the number of the beast (REV. 13:15-18).

Satan, the Antichrist, and the False Prophet, with the aid of their devotees, will all be seeking to ensure that a carpenter from Nazareth does not receive the call from the descendants of Abraham, Isaac and Jacob, "blessed is he who comes in the Name of The Lord" (MATT. 23:37-39).

---

[127] Jewish Voice, "Update on the Building of the Third Temple," *Jewish Voice*, https://www.jewishvoice.org/read/article/update-building-third-temple; Tezyapar, "New Muslim vision for Temple Mount," *Ynetnews*, https://www.ynetnews.com/articles/0,7340,L-4355421,00.html; Mizrahi, "Why the Red Heifer?" *Congregation Adat Reyim*, https://www.adatreyim.org/divrei-torah.html.

[128] Prince, "And Then the End Shall Come, Pt 2," *Derek Prince*, December 6, 2012, video, 58:02, https://youtu.be/SX7EKSMvhkA.

The Final Candidates

Before we continue with our chosen seven, I will first explain my reasoning for any exclusions, as well as potential replacements. My aim is to narrow down the criteria that binds the seven kings, from which I can find the most promising candidates, and most importantly, the *eighth king*. Each of the kings I have selected align with the seven kingdoms represented in the visions of Daniel and John (DAN. 2; 7; REV. 13; 17) and are all eschatologically relevant to the eighth king, the Antichrist, either through characteristic(s) or works they carried out. These include, but are not limited to, the propagation of idol worship in Israel, direct persecution, the brokering of temporary peace and unification in the land, and the erecting of the Temple. Our eighth king will embody the good and evil characteristics of the seven kings and utilise them for his push for ultimate control and victory. The seven can be said to provide a composite image of this beast to come. Each of these Antichrist figures opposed the God of creation, as well as the Hebrew people, and—with the exception of Cyrus—tried to dominate or destroy them. They exploited the fact that the Hebrew people held the Temple ground sacred, and either sought to destroy it or take over its authority. I believe the eighth king will do what none other has done to date—enter the Most Holy Place and in a proclamation of his God status, take a seat on the throne and be worshipped universally and exclusively.

Image 5.2 – The potential candidates for the seven kings of Revelation 17 connected with the four beasts of Daniel 7.

PERSONAL CANDIDATES FOR THE SEVEN KINGS WITH THE FOUR BEASTS		
KING(S)	KINGDOM	BEAST
Pharaoh (potentially Ramesses II)	Egypt	
Sennacherib, Ithobaal I, Hiram I	Assyria or Phoenicia	
Nimrod, Nebuchadnezzar	Babylon	1. Lion
Cyrus	Medo-Persia	2. Bear
Antiochus Epiphanes, Alexander	Greece	3. Leopard

Domitian, Hadrian	Rome	4. Combination
Hitler, or possibly a future king	Rome reformed	4. Second fulfilment

As I proceed with my list of candidates, I will consider how each king contributes to the composite image of the eighth king, the Antichrist. There must be some element of their character or actions which is to be recapitulated with the eighth king—he must truly be of the seven, the embodiment of all their ungodliness. With that said, to narrow down these kings, we will need to think outside the box to make everything fit inside the box and align with all biblical requirements.

Please refer to the footnotes to see the honourable mentions for the seven kings which I felt deserved a mention but did not necessarily fit as well as the other kings from the seven kingdoms.[129] With that being said, now it is time to put forward

---

[129] The three honourable mentions for the final seven candidates are:
Nebuchadnezzar II (Babylon) who "conquered Egypt, and Syria, and Phoenicia, and Arabia; and exceeded in his exploits all that had reigned before him in Babylon and Chaldea" (Josephus Against Apion 1:19.133). He is known as the head of gold from the great statue of Daniel 2. He was exceptionally cruel and sadistic and took delight in his power over others. The Talmud teaches that while Nebuchadnezzar reigned "no laughter emerged from any creature." Even his most fearsome General Nabzaradon trembled in fear of his master while he was still far away (Sanhedrin 96 b). He conquered Tyre and Assyria and therefore could be called a King of Tyre and the Assyrian. He also conquered Judah and led them in captivity to Babylon (Josephus, Against Apion 1.19:132). He exalted himself as a god, demanding his subjects bow down to him, in the form of a huge statue of himself, which bore the number 666, erected on the plains of Shinar (Dan. 3:1-6). But after a time of judgement under the hand of God, he repented and acknowledged the Most High as the true God. That he willingly and openly humbled himself by not only acknowledging the Most High as creator, but as the source of his gifts and power, casts doubt on his candidacy (Dan. 4:34-37).
Alexander the Great (Greece) who represented the belly of bronze on the Great Statue (Dan. 2). Alexander did not need to conquer Jerusalem by force because the Jews submitted to his rule by choice. There does not seem to be an adversarial relationship between Alexander and the Jewish people. According to Josephus, Alexander experienced a vision in which the God of Israel directed him against his enemies and saw the High Priest of Israel. When Alexander

our candidates and assess them against the profile we compiled. Let us proceed in the chronological order of the seven kingdoms (the kingdom of Babylon is placed in the time of Nebuchadnezzar, the head of gold from the great statue). The one exception to this order is our final candidate, and that is for what I believe to be a good reason.

1. Pharaoh (potentially Ramesses II) (Egypt)
Refused to release God's people from bondage and thus suffered plagues

The Pharaoh of Egypt was the main antagonist of the Israelites in the story of their bondage in Egypt and subsequent deliverance at the hand of God. The historical identity of this particular Pharaoh is not certain, but it is not required for our endeavour at hand when the biblical account of his character and actions is clear. In saying this, scholars and historians tend to side with Ramesses II, often regarded as the greatest Pharaoh from the greatest period of Egypt, the New Kingdom. In the biblical account, the family of Joseph settled in Goshen, the best part of the land and the residence of the Pharaoh (GEN. 45:9-10; 47). Centuries later, their Israelite descendants became enslaved in Goshen under a Pharaoh who treated them with great contempt and cruelty (EXOD. 5). The Israelite slaves were forced to build the store-cities of Rameses and Pithom (EXOD. 1:11). Notably, both of these historical

---

visited Jerusalem, he noticed the High Priest Jaddus from his dream, and after being shown great respect from the Jews, and being shown Hebrew scripture relating to himself, he recognised the greatness of the God of Israel (livius.org Alexander the Great visits Jerusalem).

Domitian (Rome) who was the Roman Emperor from 81-96 AD, succeeding his brother Titus who was known, along with their father Vespasian, for the destruction of Jerusalem. There is the possibility that Domitian had a hand in the death of his brother Titus to help his ascent to the throne. To rise to power by means of intrigue is indeed a sign of the eighth king. As he was the emperor *who was* during the authorship of the book of Revelation, we have to consider him a candidate. He was the first emperor to call himself "God the Lord" and "Lord of the Earth." Eusebius recorded that Domitian persecuted the Jews and Christians, but there is a lack of consensus among modern historians on the extent of this persecution. Was unable to find any occult or Rabbinical commentaries on Domitian and therefore dropped him as a serious contender.

cities (Pi-Ramesses and Per-Atum) were established by Pharaoh Ramesses II as supply sites for the military campaign in the Levant. The city of Pi-Ramesses (translates to House of Ramesses) was the capital and principal residence of Pharaoh Ramesses II to better conduct military and political affairs.[130] This aligns perfectly with the biblical story of the Israelites escaping from the grips of the Pharaoh in their exodus departure from the city of Rameses (Exod. 12:37; Num. 33:3-5).

Son of the False Light

The name Ramesses means "Ra [sun god] is the one who bore him," identifying himself as a son of the false light, Lucifer, and he came to be known by his successors as "Great Ancestor," a prototype king. The Babylonian Talmud states that he is one of four kings who exalted themselves as God, along with Sennacherib, Nebuchadnezzar and Hiram I, who are all candidates on this list.[131] To promote his self-deification throughout the kingdom he erected more status, monuments, and temples in his honour than any other Pharaoh of Egypt. This clearly alludes to his grandiose character and unwillingness to acknowledge God as his source of power and authority.

Pharaoh exalted himself as god and therefore challenged the authority of the true God by refusing to release the Israelites from bondage (Exod. 7:1-4). He himself said: "Who is the Lord, that I should obey His voice to let Israel go? I do not know the Lord, nor will I let Israel go" (V. 5:2). To try and persuade the Pharaoh of His divinity, God used Aaron to perform the miracle of transforming his staff into a snake, but Pharaoh's magicians duplicated the miracle (Vv. 7:8-12). The Pharaoh rejected the Lord and His preliminary act of grace and remained hardened in heart (Exod. 4:21-23; 7:13). God had no other choice but to inflict Egypt with the

---

[130] Isbouts, "Who was the Egyptian pharoah challenged Moses?" *National Geographic*, https://www.nationalgeographic.com/culture/people-in-the-bible/pharaoh-king-punished-god/.

[131] Babylonian Talmud Chullin 89a (ed. William Davidson Talmud).

plagues to bring the Pharaoh to repentance (Vv. 7-11). After each consecutive plague, the Pharaoh rejected God more than the last, demonstrating a rejection not of His existence, but of God Himself (EXOD. 7:13, 23; 8:15, 19; 9:34). It was not until after the tenth plague that God's people were finally liberated from the iron grip of Pharaoh. The Egyptian army pursued the fleeing Israelites into the Red Sea and were engulfed by it while the Israelites passed to the other side (EXOD. 14). The Israelites acknowledged the mighty hand of the Lord and "put their trust in him and in Moses his servant" (Vv. 14:31). They had started their spiritual preparation to enter the kingdom of God.

Recapitulation of the Exodus under a Greater Pharaoh

There will be a recapitulation of the Exodus narrative during the period of great tribulation under the kingdom of the Antichrist (DAN. 12:1; MATT. 24:21-22). Like the Pharaoh, he will exalt himself above the Most High and refuse to release the Israelites from his bondage. The miraculous works of the two witnesses will be disregarded by the multitudes because of the supernatural powers of the Antichrist and the False Prophet. God will send plagues upon the earth to seek a change of heart and spiritual direction from mankind. Following this divine warning, God will inflict judgement on the world as He did on Egypt because of the rebellion of the Antichrist and his unrepentant allies (PSA. 2). The plagues sent upon the world to call man to repentance fit a similar progression and nature to the plagues in Egypt (REV. 6; 8; 9; 16). Egypt experienced the plague of total darkness for three days, just prior to the judgement on the first born, and the miraculous sparing of the Israelites. This led to the destruction of Egypt's armies as they chased the Israelites into the Red Sea. Jesus declared that prior to the outpoured wrath of God there will be a time of total darkness, the conclusion of which will herald in the miraculous rapturing of his Church to save them from the wrath to come (1 THESS. 5:1-11; 2 THESS. 1:5-10). The trials and tribulations will conclude in the same manner as in Egypt, with the victory of Christ over the Antichrist and the destruction of his armies at the battle of Armageddon. The people left on earth who turn to God will be liberated from the iron grip of the Antichrist and be spiritually prepared to join Jesus Christ in the messianic kingdom. The song of deliverance Moses and the Israelites sang to the Lord after coming out of the Red Sea (EXOD. 15:1-20) will be sung again after the time of God's wrath along with a new song of deliverance to the Lamb (REV. 15:1-4). Having entered into the full inheritance of the new covenant promised to them (JER. 31:31-37), the Jews will remember a greater deliverance than that in Egypt:

> *"However, the days are coming," declares the Lord, "when it will no longer be said, 'As surely as the Lord lives, who brought the Israelites up out of Egypt,' but it will be said, 'As surely as the Lord lives, who brought the Israelites up out of the land of the north and out of all the countries where he had banished them.' For I will restore them to the land I gave their ancestors (Jer. 16:14-15 NIV).*

As restated in Jeremiah 23, the Israelites will never again refer to the deliverance under Moses, but the deliverance under the prophet greater than Moses who is called The Lord our Righteousness (JER. 23:3-8). Remarkably, Jeremiah said of this great deliverance that the name given to Judah and Jerusalem, the seat of the throne of this king, will be "The Lord our Righteousness" (JER. 33:10-26). This highlights the fact that the false Pharaoh has been forever banished. Quite obviously the current return from their banishment among the nations has not yet elicited this proclamation from Israel and the Jewish people, therefore the current return has not fulfilled the requirements of the prophecies just stated. They will be fulfilled under a greater Pharaoh yet to arise and the true king who will destroy him.

Image 5.3 – Parallels of the plagues wrought on Egypt to those which are to come during the final tribulation.

PLAGUE	EGYPT	FINAL TRIBULATION
Water turned to blood	Ex. 7:20-24; Psa. 105:29	Rev. 8:8-9; 11:6; 16:3-6
Frogs	Ex. 8:6; Psa. 105:30	Rev. 16:13-14
Lice	Ex. 8:17; Psa. 105:31	Rev. 11:6
Flies	Ex. 8:21-24; Psa. 105:31	Rev. 11:6
Pestilence	Ex. 9:1-6; Psa. 105:35	Rev. 6:8; 8:9
Boils	Ex. 9:10	Rev. 16:1-2
Hail and fire	Ex. 9:22-26; Psa. 105:32	Rev. 8:7; 16:21
Locusts	Ex. 10:12-15; Psa. 105:34	Rev. 9:3-4
Darkness	Ex. 10:21-23; Psa. 105:28	Rev. 8:12; 9:2; 16:10-11
Death of Firstborn	Ex. 11:4-8; 12:29; Psa. 105:36	Rev. 19:19-21

2. Sennacherib (Assyria)

Directly challenged God and His Holy Jerusalem so God retaliated by destroying his army in a single day and saving Jerusalem

Sennacherib was king of the Assyrian Empire and the destroyer of the Kingdom of Israel. As king, Sennacherib crushed many neighbouring countries before setting his sights on the Kingdom of Israel. Because the Israelites were persistent in their unbelief and their transgressions of the covenant, God allowed Israel to be delivered into Sennacherib's hands (2 KGS. 18:11-12). Sennacherib continued to the Kingdom of Judah in the south and claimed most of its cities (2 KGS. 18:13; 2 CHR. 32; ISA. 36:1). Before reaching Jerusalem, Sennacherib taunted the God of Israel by telling the Jews to surrender their faith in God for He was no different to all the other gods who failed to deliver their peoples from the wrath of Sennacherib (2 KGS. 18:28-35; 2 CHR. 32:9-19; ISA. 36:13-20). In response, Hezekiah prayed before the Lord for Him to hear the blasphemous words of Sennacherib and save His people from destruction so that all the world may know their Lord is God (2 KGS. 19:14-19; 2 CHR. 32:20; ISA. 37:14-20). That same night the Lord answered by sending an angel to strike down 185,000 in the Assyrian camp (2 KGS. 19:20-

36; 2 CHR. 32:21; ISA. 37:21-37). Sennacherib promptly withdrew his siege of Jerusalem and departed for Nineveh in Babylon, never to return (2 KGS. 19:36).

Jerusalem's Prayers will be Answered Again

The eighth king, the Antichrist, who possesses the abilities of all the seven kings, will succeed where Sennacherib could not by entering the glorious city of Jerusalem by means of peace. He will assume authority over Jerusalem and the Temple and then seek to destroy the Jews and erase the memory of their God, along with all other gods, like Sennacherib did. In the final days of judgement when the Jews enter into the final year of celebrating the fall feasts of the Lord and they observe the Days of Awe (the Ten Days of Repentance), they will plead to God to save them from destruction at the hands of the Antichrist. This period of deep mourning and internal reflection will finally soften their hardened hearts to the Word of God, and they will weep greatly over their rejection of Jesus Christ (ZECH. 12:1-14). God, who patiently waited for His people to accept Him will answer their prayers, and after the final day for repentance on the Day of Atonement, supernaturally slay the armies of the Antichrist in one day as he did to the armies of Sennacherib (REV. 19:11-21). No one among the nations will doubt or deny the God of Israel any longer, and all of His people will be saved from destruction.

3. Ithobaal I (Phoenicia-Assyria)
Infiltrated Israel with Baal Worship

Ithobaal I (meaning with Baal) was a king of Tyre who expanded the territorial reach of the kingdom to include all of Phoenicia, including Sidon. He is mentioned in the Bible as being the "king of Sidon" (1 KGS. 16.31). The ancient historian Menander of Ephesus recorded that Ithobaal I murdered the previous king, Pheles, to capture the throne.[132] The Antichrist will snatch the throne in a

---

[132] Josephus, "Against Apion," 1.116.

similar act of intrigue and "pluck up" three of the ten kings in the world empire (DAN 7:8, 24). Menander continued that Ithobaal I worshipped the Phoenician gods to the fullest, serving as a priest of Astarte, the Phoenician goddess of war and love, known as the Queen of Heaven (Semiramis).[133] The Queen of Heaven was identified with Venus, the evening and morning star—alluding to Lucifer, to whom he was ultimately committed. This goddess still figures prominently in our present world, and is commonly associated with Mary, the mother of Jesus, though neither herself, nor her God, ever conferred such a title upon her.

Following the footsteps of his great ancestor Hiram I who corrupted the Davidic kingdom by leading King Solomon into the sinful behaviour of the Phoenicians, Ithobaal I introduced Baal worship directly into the kingship of Israel (1 KGS. 16:31). To infiltrate God's earthly kingdom, Ithobaal I established close diplomatic ties with King Ahab of Israel and solidified the relationship by marrying off his wicked daughter Jezebel to King Ahab (1 KGS. 16:31). With this move the Phoenicians and the Israelites became intertwined politically and biologically. The Phoenician influence penetrated the Kingdom of Judah only one generation later when Athaliah, the daughter of Ahab and Jezebel, married King Joram of Judah (2 KGS. 8:18; 11:18). The kingdoms of Israel and Judah became corrupted to their core and would never recover. Sennacherib destroyed the Kingdom of Israel and Nebuchadnezzar destroyed the Kingdom of Judah for their perpetual disobedience towards God and reverence towards Baal (JER. 32:30-35; 2 KGS. 25:1-10).

It was said of Ahab that no king before him had committed more wickedness in the sight of the Lord due to the Phoenician influence of his wife Jezebel (1 KGS. 16:30-33; 21:25-26). Working as agents of Ithobaal, Jezebel and King Ahab instituted Baal worship through the kingdom of Israel, erected false idols and temples to

---

[133] Ibid., 1.118.

Baal throughout all of Israel, and tried to eradicate all traces of Yahweh worship by force (1 KGS. 16:30-33; 18:3-4; 19:10, 14).

This will be taken to its limit during the coming period of tribulation when the Antichrist infiltrates Israel with ungodly worship towards himself, the human manifestation of Baal. When Elijah challenged the 450 prophets of Baal during the reign of Ahab, Elijah was the only prophet of God left in Israel (1 KGS. 18:22; 19:10, 14). Even still, it was the God of Israel, not Baal, who answered the call of Elijah with fire from heaven, and all the people turned away from Baal and destroyed the priests (1 KGS. 18:16-40). Elijah will return in the end days with Moses as the two witnesses to again challenge the allies of the Antichrist (REV. 11; MATT. 17:3-4; MAL. 4:5). They will force the people to reconsider their allegiance to the Antichrist with divine works and supernatural abilities. After they are killed by the beast, they will resurrect three-and-a-half days later and ascend to heaven before the masses (REV. 11:3-13).

4. Nimrod (Babylon)

Consolidated world power to challenge God

We have previously discussed the character and actions of Nimrod at great length in the second chapter. What is important to stress about Nimrod in relation to the seven kings is his status as the prototypical king in opposition to God. Each of the seven kings follow the example established by Nimrod. His kingdom which began at Babel is likewise the prototypical ungodly kingdom (GEN. 10:10-11).

Could Nimrod be the Assyrian whom we have associated with the Antichrist? (MIC. 5:6; EZEK. 31:3; ISA. 10:5, 25; 14:25; 31:8). The prophet Micah talked about a coming godly ruler who will be great until the ends of the earth (Messiah) and will be the peace of his people when the Assyrian comes into their land (MIC. 5:1-5). In that day, the land of Assyria and Nimrod (Shinar) will be devastated and all of God's enemies cut off (MIC. 5:6-15). Modern translations state that it was Nimrod who founded the Assyrian empire in the city of Asshur and built the cities of Nineveh, Rehoboth, Calah, and

Resen. However, the Septuagint and Vulgate translations of the Bible, as well as Jubilees and Josephus, state that Asshur, presumably the son of Shem, was its founder (GEN. 10:8-12; JUB. 9:3).[134] The difficulty lies in designating the usage of Asshur as an individual or as the name for the city. Asshur did in fact come to be known as the founding city of the Assyrians and at one time, its capital city. If the modern translations are indeed correct, it could mean Nimrod is the head of the Assyrians and could rightly be called *the Assyrian*.

Is Nimrod Only a Prototype?

The most famous and important of the legends in Freemasonry which underpins the ceremony for the Masonic Master Mason degree, the Third Degree, appears to be linked to Nimrod in his reincarnated or born-again form of Tammuz. The story behind the ceremony is derived from details in the Bible on the building of the First Temple (1 KGS. 5-7; 2 CHR. 2-4). It deals with the theme of death, burial and resurrection through the biblical character Hiram Abiff. Hiram Abiff is the first, and in most jurisdictions, the only named character a candidate ever has to re-enact as part of the Master Mason ceremony. But who in fact is being raised? In the legend, three craftsmen working on the Temple demand Hiram Abiff to divulge the secrets of the craft and end up killing him for his refusal to comply. King Solomon and King Hiram of Tyre hurry to the Temple where his body is buried and seeing the Master Mason dead, realise his secrets have perished with him. They become desperate to bring him back to life. Solomon finally succeeds in resurrecting Hiram Abiff by grabbing his right hand with the "strong grip of the Lion's paw," a Masonic hand grip.

> "This story, based on the Masonic legend of Hiram Abiff, is acted out for every Master Mason initiate with the candidate unwittingly playing the part of Hiram. The

---

[134] Josephus, "Antiquities of the Jews," 1.143.

> *Master Mason initiation re-enacts the legend of Osiris and Horus or Nimrod and Tammuz. Hiram Abiff as the widow's son represents Tammuz, son of the widow Semiramus. Widowed by Nimrod's death, Semiramus declared Tammuz to be resurrected or born-again Nimrod."[135]*

It appears here that the legend actually relates to the resurrected Nimrod, who is hinted at as being the God of Philosophy to reappear. The leading Masonic leaders all confess this legend is an allegory that only hints at the truth, and only the adepts (Masons who have reached the higher degrees, up to the 33rd Degree) are shown the true meaning. I personally believe this to be a diversion in the same way the archetypal legends surrounding Nimrod are diversions or counterfeits of the resurrection of Jesus and of the trinity. Deception or diversion is a common tool used by the leading Masons to mislead even the lower-level Masons in their ranks. In his book *Morals and Dogma*, prominent Freemason Albert Pike wrote that Masonry "conceals it secrets from all except the Adepts and Sages, or the Elect, and uses false explanations and misinterpretations of its symbols to mislead ... to conceal the Truth, which it calls Light."[136] Pike explained this process in great detail:

> *"The Blue Degrees are but the outer court or portico of the Temple. Part of the symbols are displayed there to the Initiate, but he is intentionally misled by false interpretations. It is not intended that he shall understand them; but it is intended that he shall imagine he understands them. Their true explication is reserved for the Adepts, the Princes of Masonry. The whole body of the Royal and Sacerdotal Art was hidden so carefully,*

[135] Peacock, "The Harlot and the Church," *Garden Place Ministries*, http://myplace.frontier.com/~arlenpeacock/harlotandthechurch.html.

[136] Pike, *Morals and Dogma*, 104-105.

centuries since, in the High Degrees, as that it is even yet impossible to solve many of the enigmas which they contain. It is well enough for the mass of those called Masons, to imagine that all is contained in the Blue Degrees; and whoso attempts to undeceive them will labor in vain, and without any true reward violate his obligations as an Adept.[137]

According to the Virginia Royal Arch Masons, "the Hiramic Legend became a part of Masonic Traditions between 1723 and 1738, and not earlier" after the Third Degree was first conferred in 1724.[138] They state how "there is no mention of Hiram Abiff in the Old Charges," the foundational Masonic documents, until the "second Constitutions of 1738." Perhaps it is an example of this deceptive practice in play to hide the true Masonic understanding of who this dying and rising figure truly is. Could it be the God of Philosophy, the Truth and the Light? A new legend seems to have been developed, perhaps as a means of obfuscation to divert researchers from the truth behind the allegory. Again, I believe the allusions to Nimrod through Tammuz and Hiram Abiff as the coming king are merely as a prototype.

5. King Cyrus the Great (Medo-Persia)
Peace-broker who gave the decree to rebuild the Temple

Cyrus the Great founded the Achaemenid empire, the first of the Persian empires, after conquering the Medes, Babylonians, and Lydians. He, along with King Darius the Mede whom he conquered, are pictured as the chest and arms of silver on the great statue (DAN. 2). King Cyrus was sympathetic to the cause of his Jewish subjects, having been directly anointed by God (by his name Cyrus) over a century before he was born to subdue their

---

[137] Ibid., 819.

[138] Bundy, "Allegories of Hiram Abiff," Virginia Royal Arch Research Chapter no. 1753,
https://virginiaroyalarch.org/education/pdfs/Allegories_of_Hiram_Abiff.pdf.

oppressors-to-come and liberate them from captivity (ISA. 44:26-28; 45:1-6).[139] Again, God made provisions for deliverance before judgement was meted out. As per the prophetic writings, it was Cyrus who made the decree for the Jews to return to their homeland and rebuild the Temple and the holy city of Jerusalem (ISA. 44:28; 45:1-13; EZRA 1; 4:1-5; 5:13-17; 6:3-5; 2 CHR. 36:22-23).[140]

As with all of his subjects, Cyrus preserved and respected the religious and cultural traditions of the Jews, a stance which the Jews appreciated greatly. To this day, Cyrus is recognised by the Jews at large as a great liberator and a gentile anointed by God. It may seem strange to place Cyrus in the list of candidates for the seven kings in light of his reverential status, but I believe it to be necessary for the Antichrist to embody these elements of Cyrus. How else could he garner widespread Jewish and gentile support for a comprehensive Middle East peace?

Like Cyrus, the Antichrist will subdue the world before him and restore order from the chaos of religious divisions around the world. The covenant of peace will include a clause for the Jews to rebuild the Temple in Jerusalem with the approval of their Muslim neighbours. He will foster an attitude of acceptance between the world religions and encourage an ecumenical unity, but unlike under Cyrus, his intentions will be nefarious. Incorporating the qualities of the seven kings, the Antichrist will exploit the consolidation of religious worship by diverting all worship to himself within the Temple of God (DAN. 11:21-24). In a 2018 public address, Prime Minister of Israel, Benjamin Netanyahu, seemed to foreshadow the coming acceptance of a gentile leader in the character of Cyrus:

> *I want to tell you that the Jewish people have a long memory, so we remember the proclamation of the great king, Cyrus the Great, the Persian king 2,500 years ago. He proclaimed that the Jewish exiles in Babylon could*

---

[139] Josephus, "Antiquities of the Jews," 11.1-8.

[140] Ibid.; Josephus, "Against Apion," 1.128-132.

> *come back and rebuild our Temple in Jerusalem ... And
> we remember how a few weeks ago, President Donald J.
> Trump recognized Jerusalem as Israel's capital. Mr.
> President, this will be remembered by our people
> through the ages.*[141]

How much more will the eighth king be exalted when he restores
Jerusalem into Jewish hands and allows them to rebuild the
Temple like King Cyrus?

6. Antiochus Epiphanes (Greece)
The Little Horn who desolated the Temple

Antiochus Epiphanes was king of the Greek Seleucid Empire, one
of the four divisions (horns) of the Greek-Macedonian Empire
after the death of Alexander the Great (DAN. 8; 11:2-4). Because of the
many similarities, Antiochus Epiphanes is commonly identified as
the little horn said to come forth from one of these four kingdoms
(DAN. 8; 1 MAC. 1). Matching the prophetic vision of Daniel, Antiochus
seized the throne by illegitimate and deceptive means (DAN. 8:8-9,
21-25; 11:21-23), usurping the legitimate heir Demetrius I Soter who
was held hostage in Rome.[142]

Antiochus, taking up the epitaph Epiphanes, meaning *God
Manifest*, reckoned himself to be the human manifestation of
Zeus, the chief deity of the Greek pantheon of gods. In accordance
with this self-estimation, Antiochus desired all of his subjects
within the kingdom to worship Zeus (himself) and the rest of the
Greek pantheon. Like the Antichrist who holds himself in even
higher esteem, Antiochus contended that "all should be one people
and that all should give up their particular customs" (1 MAC. 1:41-42).
This of course was no suggestion, but an order to follow the
Hellenic customs at the threat of death (1 MAC. 1:41-63; 2 MAC. 6:7-11).

---

[141] Silow-Carroll, "Who is King Cyrus, and why did Netanyahu compare him to
Trump?" *Times of Israel*, https://www.timesofisrael.com/who-is-king-cyrus-
and-why-is-netanyahu-comparing-him-to-trump/.

[142] Miller, *Daniel*, vol. 18 of *New American Commentary*, 225.

The entirety of the law and the holy books were to be *forcibly* forgotten (1 Mac. 1:49). No longer could they make offerings in the Temple, follow the sabbaths, celebrate festivals, or practice circumcision (1 Mac. 1:44-50). Anyone who possessed the book of the law or "adhered to the law was condemned to death by decree of the king" (1 Mac. 1:56-57).[143] Entire families were murdered if the children were found to be circumcised (1 Mac. 1:60). Antiochus auctioned off the role of High Priest to the highest bidder willing to promote his own purposes, regardless of their tribe or qualifications (2 Mac. 4:7-15, 23-25). The entire priesthood followed suit and abandoned their priestly services to celebrate the Greek culture (2 Mac. 4:13-15).

When Antiochus heard a false report of a revolt in Judah, he elevated the levels of persecution to unparalleled heights by commanding his soldiers to attack Judah and massacre everyone in sight, young and old (1 Mac. 1:29-32; 2 Mac. 5:11-14). His goal was to destroy "the remnant of Jerusalem" and "banish the memory of them from the place" (1 Mac. 3:32-36). After only three days, 80,000 were killed and just as many were sold into slavery (2 Mac. 5:14).

Antiochus himself entered the Temple and took for himself all of its treasure, the golden altar, the lampstand, and all the utensils used for the sacred rituals (1 Mac. 1:20-24; 2 Mac. 5:15-16). Upon returning to Antioch with the spoils, he once again ordered an army of 22,000 to return to Jerusalem and "kill all the grown men and to sell the women and boys as slaves" (2 Mac. 5:21-26). Abominable altars, shrines, and facilities were erected all throughout Judah and sacrilegious offerings were made in the Temple itself (1 Mac. 1:14, 46-47, 54-55, 59). The Temple was turned away from worship to Yahweh and rededicated to Zeus (himself). Inside the Temple he erected a statue of Zeus in his own likeness and sacrificed unclean animals on the altar. Prostitution, sexual intercourse, and all types of debauchery were means of sanctification inside the Temple (2 Mac. 6:1-5). He had successfully

---

[143] Josephus, "The Wars of the Jews," 1.34.

corrupted the people to forsake the covenant to God through acts of flattery (DAN. 11:31-32; 1 MAC. 2:18; 2 MAC. 7:24). This event is known as the abomination of desolation in the book of Daniel (DAN. 8:11-13; 9:27; 11:31; 12:11), and it is what set off the successful Maccabean revolt which brought a brief period of Jewish independence (2 MAC. 8-10).[144] These were the God-fearing people who Daniel knew would "carry out great exploits" (DAN. 11:31-35).

Antiochus as Little Horn Analysed

It is safe to say that Antiochus lived up to the prophecy of the little horn as a cunning deceiver and destroyer of the holy people through his self-exaltation (DAN. 8:23-25). In his commentary on the book of Revelation for the *Daily Study Bible*, William Barclay emphasised the Antichrist comparison:

> "*History has seldom, or never, seen so deliberate attempt to wipe out the faith and religion of a whole people.*" He continued that "*to the Jews Antiochus was the incarnation of all evil; he is the blasphemous little horn of Daniel; he is the nearest approach to Antichrist in human form.*"[145]

But when we consider the totality of the prophecy on the little horn, it is clear Antiochus Epiphanes is only a partial fulfilment, or type, of the greater little horn to come, the Antichrist. First, take the description of the little horn as rising "against the Prince of princes" and being "broken without human means" (DAN. 8:25). If we accept the testimony from Maccabees, he was indeed broken by God, who smote him with an incurable disease (1 MAC. 6:8-13; 2 MAC. 9:5-29). But to me, this description applies better to the Antichrist due to the biblical evidence. It is he who embodies the feet of the great statue (DAN. 2) which is shattered by the rock "made not with human hands," but by God (DAN. 2:34-35). He and his

---

144 Ibid., 1.31-38.

145 Barclay, *The Revelation of John*, 73.

armies are truly "broken without human means" by the rock, the kingdom of Christ, which is then inaugurated for an eternal reign (DAN. 2:44-45).

Second, Professor Mark Hassler rightly contended that the little horn which is said to "wax exceedingly great" cannot ultimately be Antiochus because of his comparatively weak and incomplete triumphs to the ram and the goat (DAN. 8:9). Antiochus did not "accumulate more territory than the ram" which is required from the prophecy:

> *"The ram, goat, and little horn each 'magnify or enlarge' their territory—the latter two more so than the former. Antiochus cannot be the little horn because he amassed less country than the ram. As Shea reasons, "Antiochus IV should have exceeded the Persian and Greek Empires in greatness. Obviously, this was not the case, since he ruled only one portion of the Grecian Empire with but little success."*[146]

Indeed, it is said that the goat with the large horn (Greek empire and Alexander the Great) grew "very great," but the little horn (Antiochus) grew "exceedingly great" (DAN. 8:8-9). What king fitting all the prophecies from Daniel could possibly exceed the achievements of Alexander if not the Antichrist to come?

When it comes to Daniel 11, both liberal and conservative scholars have no trouble relating verses 21-35 to Antiochus Epiphanes, but those which remain do not align with our understanding of him (DAN. 11:36-45). Two distinct figures are depicted in these two fragments. Theologian Daniel Akin noted how it is an example of "prophetic foreshortening" where there is a significant time interval between neighbouring verses.[147] He

---

[146] Hassler, "The Identity of the Little Horn," *Master's Seminary Journal* 27, no. 1 (Spring 2016): 36.

[147] Akin, "Antiochus Epiphanes and Antichrist," Danny Akins, http://www.danielakin.com/wp-content/uploads/2017/01/Daniel-11.21-45-

mentions how this technique is present in Jesus' interpretation of Isaiah 61:1-2, where he "proclaims the year of the Lord's favor" but leaves the reading of the "day of vengeance" for his second coming. The seventy weeks determined before the end in Daniel 9 contains a similar gap between the fulfilment of the first sixty-nine weeks (DAN. 9:24-26) from the final week in the time of Antichrist rule (DAN. 9:27). To bring this together, the first fragment speaks to the past, "the appointed time" in reference to Antiochus (VV. 27, 29, 35), and the "end of time" in the second fragment (VV. 40; 12:1-13) speaks to the future, the time of the Antichrist. As an example, in the Antichrist fragment, it is said "he shall regard neither the God of his fathers ... nor any god; for he shall exalt himself above them all" (VV. 36). But we know Antiochus did not forsake the God of his fathers; all of his life he enforced the worship of the Greek pantheon along with himself, the self-proclaimed human manifestation of Zeus.

Antiochus then, presents a partial image of the coming eighth king, the Antichrist, who will fit all of the prophetic descriptors from Daniel as the little horn (DAN. 7; 8:9-14, 23-26), the coming prince (DAN. 9:26-27), and the despicable person who ascends to power through intrigue (DAN. 11-21).[148] He will likewise desecrate the Third Temple and exalt himself above the Most High God (DAN. 8:11-13, 25; 11:31-37; 12:11). When Jesus referenced the abomination of desolation from Daniel, he warned of its recapitulation by the Antichrist to come. He was not speaking of the "appointed time" in relation to Antiochus, but the "time of the end," the time of the great tribulation under the Antichrist (MATT. 24:15-21; MARK 13:14-19; LUKE 21:20-24). Paul also referenced this prophecy in terms of its future fulfilment by the Antichrist, the man of sin (2 THESS. 2:3-4; DAN. 11:31-37). The people will be forced to make a similar choice between God and the ways of the Antichrist. Just as the Maccabees raised up a revolt against Antiochus and reclaimed Jerusalem and

---

Antiochus-Epiphanes-and-Antichrist.-The-Arch-Enemies-of-Gods-People-manuscript-kh.pdf.

[148] Hassler, "The Identity of the Little Horn," 44.

rededicated the Temple, Jesus will replay these events on his return (1-2 MAC.).[149] Jesus is to defeat the armies of Antichrist, liberate Jerusalem, build up the Temple of the Church, and bring God's glory over all the earth (MATT. 24:29-31; ZECH. 14:2-9; 40-43; HAB. 2:14).

7. Hadrian (Rome)
Persecuted and Expelled the Jews from Jerusalem

Hadrian was a Roman emperor during the height of its power, reigning from 117-138 AD. He is known as one of the greatest adversaries of the Jews. The Rabbis called him a "type of a pagan king" for his reign of great persecution, and for expelling the Jews from Jerusalem after the Bar Kokhba revolt.[150] The ramifications of these actions are felt even today. It has not even been a hundred years since the Jews returned to the land. Ever since this time their neighbours have sought to annihilate them and constantly barrage them with attacks from all fronts.

Hadrian "was deeply involved in witchcraft and occultic ceremonies" as a member of the secret mysteries of Eleusis, a precursor of Freemasonry, where inductees swore their lives away to secrecy. David Cloud considered the founding myth of the society, "a cheap demonic substitute for the incarnation, atonement, and resurrection of Christ."[151] Not surprisingly, Hadrian's mother was born in Phoenicia, the launchpad for ungodliness, in the city of Gades, which fittingly means *holy base* or *he is the sun Lord.*[152] It was in Gades where the Pillars of Hercules were established. The renowned ancient Greek historian Herodotus equated Hercules with the Phoenician god Melquart

---

[149] Josephus, "The Wars of the Jews," 1.31-38.

[150] Genesis Rabbah 63:7.

[151] Cloud, "Hadrian: The Enemy of God," *Way of Life Literature*, https://www.wayoflife.org/reports/hadrian_the_enemy_of_god.php.

[152] Wasson, "Gades," Ancient History Encyclopedia, https://www.ancient.eu/Gades/.

(Molech), another example of Baal worship pervading the line of seven kings.

Hadrian desired to blot out the worship of Yahweh and his people just like the Antichrist who intends on doing so to overturn God's judgement. Hadrian rebuilt the destroyed Jerusalem in a Romanized image, replacing the names of Israel with *Syria Palaestina* and Jerusalem with *Aelio Capitolina*. Hadrian chose to rename Israel after the Philistines (Palestine) which he knew to be enemies of the Jews. As for Jerusalem, *Aelia* is derived from Hadrian's family name Aelius, and *Capitolina* refers to the idolatrous cult of the Capitoline Triad in Rome (Jupiter, Juno, and Minerva).[153] The new city was to be dedicated to the worship of himself as emperor, the earthly manifestation of Jupiter (Zeus in Greek mythology).[154] On the ruins of the Temple Mount he raised a new temple to Jupiter (himself) with a statue of himself in the interior.[155] All throughout Jerusalem he erected similar idolatrous structures and forbade the practice of all Jewish customs.

The remnant of Jews left in Judah at the time were roused to revolt under the leadership of Bar Kokhba.[156] After initial success, the revolt was totally crushed. According to Roman historian Cassius Dio, 580,000 Jews were killed and many more died from starvation and disease, while the able-bodied were sold as slaves. Hadrian subsequently passed a law which forbade the Jews from entry into Jerusalem, and from even seeing it from a distance.[157] This calamity, or what could be considered a genocide, set in motion the Jewish scattering from their land into a diaspora.

---

[153] Cloud, "Hadrian: The Enemy of God," *Way of Life Literature*, https://www.wayoflife.org/reports/hadrian_the_enemy_of_god.php.

[154] Dio, "Roman History," 69.12.1; Henderson, *The Life and Principate of the Emperor Hadrian*, 112-113.

[155] Jerome, *Commentary on Isaiah*, 2.9.

[156] Dio, "Roman History," 69.12-15; Eusebius, "Church History," 4.6.3.

[157] Ibid.; Martyr, "First Apology," ch. 31.

Because of Hadrian, the Jews would not return until the rebirth of Israel in 1948, over 1800 years later.[158]

Eusebius noted that once "the city had been emptied of the Jewish nation and had suffered the total destruction of its ancient inhabitants; it was colonized by a different race."[159] Could this be the source of the Jewish-Palestinian conflict over the land which still rages on nearly two centuries later? The Antichrist will no doubt utilise this age-old conflict caused by Hadrian to broker peace in the Middle East and assist in his ascent to king of the world.

8. Adolf Hitler (Germany)
Systematic Jewish Genocide

Adolf Hitler was the Führer of Nazi Germany who came closer to wiping out the Jewish population than any who came before him. The Jewish genocide that he masterminded claimed the lives of an estimated six million Jews during the time of World War II, along with multitudes of other groups considered undesirable, such as Poles, gypsies, homosexuals, and those with deformities or disabilities. Even in the face of economic collapse and certain defeat, he continued in his quest to annihilate the Jews and minorities he deemed expendable.

Hitler exalted himself to godlike status and was treated as such by his people because of his extreme charisma and ability to manipulate popular sentiment. Hitler and his underlings, notably Joseph Goebbels, were pioneers in the art of state propaganda to sway public opinion and maintain absolute order. This will also be a characteristic of the Antichrist (DAN 7:20; 8:25; 11:21-24; REV. 13).

Hitler and Germany as the Seventh?
Hitler wanted to establish a thousand-year Third Reich, officially

---

[158] Ronen, "Hadrian's Curse," *Christian Friends of Israeli Communities,* https://cfoic.com/hadrians-curse/.

[159] Eusebius, "Church History," 4.6.4.

called the Greater Germanic Reich, as an ungodly alternative to the millennial kingdom under the true Messiah. The name was chosen as a direct reference to the pan-Germanic Holy Roman Empire, the First Reich, and the derivation of the Roman empire, the final of the seven kingdoms. In his book *The Dictators*, Stephen Brockmann said, "Hitler declared that the Holy Roman Empire had been 'resurrected,' although he secretly maintained his own empire to be better than the old 'Roman' one."[160] Could this point to Hitler as the seventh king said to reign only a short time before the eighth king, the Antichrist appears? If the seventh kingdom is a restored Roman Empire, perhaps the Antichrist will achieve what Hitler could not by re-establishing the Roman empire to its fullest glory.

The influence of Hitler strongly persists to this day through fascist and antisemitic sentiment. The Antichrist will both benefit from and foster these attitudes to help bring about a greater Holocaust, the time of the Great Tribulation spoken of so clearly by Jesus (MATT. 24:21-24). Could this be the connection between the seventh and the eighth kings?

Elimination of the Faith

Hitler repeatedly remarked that "in the long run, 'National Socialism and religion will no longer be able to exist together."[161] In the diaries of Joseph Goebbels, the Reich Minister of Propaganda and close confidant of Hitler, he wrote in 1939 how Hitler was "deeply religious, though completely anti-Christian," viewing it as a branch of the Jewish race which he hated.[162]

In his book *Hitler: A Biography*, history professor Ian Kershaw pointed out how as early as 1937, Hitler "was declaring that 'Christianity was ripe for destruction', and that the Churches must yield to the 'primacy of the state,'" and how Hitler was

---

[160] Brockmann, *Nuremberg: The Imaginary Capital*, 179.

[161] Overy, *The Dictators: Hitler's Germany, Stalin's Russia*, 287.

[162] Goebbels, *The Goebbels Diaries 1939-41*, 77.

against any compromise to be made with what he called "the most horrible institution imaginable."[163]

Fred Taylor mentioned how "Hitler repeatedly deprecated Christianity, and told confidants that his reluctance to make public attacks on the Church was not a matter of principle, but a pragmatic political move."[164] This was because Christianity maintained a strong influence on German society. Goebbels wrote in April 1941 that though Hitler was a fierce opponent of the Vatican and Christianity, "he forbids me [Goebbels] to leave the church. For tactical reasons."[165]

Hitler distorted the faith into a form of "positive Christianity" as a temporary compromise. In this Nazi-approved form of Christianity, all Jewish content was removed and all passages in conflict with Nazi ideology were transformed. But ultimately, even historians agree that Hitler's ultimate intention was to destroy Christianity. Shirer, the author of *The Rise and Fall of the Third Reich*, argued that the substitute was to be "the old paganism of the early tribal Germanic gods and the new paganism of the Nazi extremists.[166] There is certainly precedent for this idea. Adolf Hitler was adamant that the ancient Greeks and Romans were among the racial ancestors of the Germans. He was fervent in his support and advocacy for their "superior" culture. The *Ahnenerbe*, later called the *Research and Teaching Community of the Ancestral Heritage*, was established by Hitler as a wing of the SS in 1935 to promote these racial ideals of the Führer. Hitler, along with the elite Nazi circle, were occultists (members of Thule society) seeking a return to their "ancestral heritage" in the ancient mysteries. One such god they came to honour was the warrior shamanism of Odin (Wotan). As we previously discussed, Odin was derived from the Germanic idol Esus, another derivative of Esau, the Edomite. This was the source of the Germanic warrior

---

[163] Kershaw, *Hitler: A Biography*, 295-297.

[164] Goebbels, *The Goebbels Diaries 1939-41*, 340.

[165] Ibid.

[166] Shirer, *Rise and Fall of the Third Reich*, 240.

shamanism which dominated much of the twentieth century and caused so much bloodshed.

The Nazi symbol of the swastika was another reference back to their ancient mystery past. It was related to the Nordic myths on Odin (Edom) who is "represented as passing through space as a whirling disk or swastika looking down through all worlds."[167] The swastika was similarly used by the Phoenicians, the centre of the ancient mysteries, as a symbol of the Sun. The symbol had sacred uses for the Phoenician priestesses. The Jews in the ancient kingdoms of Israel and Judah might well have been familiar with this Nazi symbol of persecution due to the Phoenician infiltration.

The ungodly spirit which possessed the line of Esau was mythologised in his derivative, Odin, whom I believe paints the clearest picture of this spirit that will animate the Antichrist and the False Prophet. Like the Edomites, Odin is concerned only with chaos and destruction without regard for cause or consequence.[168] Destruction is not a means to an end; it is the end. This encapsulates the Luciferic rebellion in the first place. Daniel said that the Antichrist will worship no god but himself, but then paradoxically states he will worship a god of forces or fortresses, a god known to none of his predecessors (Dan. 11:36-39). This, I believe, is the worship of destruction itself, the extinguishing of the light of God and goodness. The ultimate manifestation of that evil spirit which drove Odin or Esau.

9. Hiram, King of Tyre (Phoenicia)
Builder of the Temple and Ally to the Kingdom of Israel

Hiram I was the son and successor of King Abibaal of Tyre (meaning my father is Baal) and a great ancestor of Ithobaal I. He was responsible for turning the city of Tyre into the strongest in

---

[167] Black, "The Powerful Symbol of the Swastika," *Ancient Origins*, https://www.ancient-origins.net/myths-legends/symbol-swastika-and-its-12000-year-old-history-001312.

[168] McCoy, "Odin," Norse Mythology for Smart People, https://norse-mythology.org/gods-and-creatures/the-aesir-gods-and-goddesses/odin/.

Phoenicia. The Phoenicians were excellent sailors and artisans who developed trade extensively throughout the Mediterranean. This led to a strong trade alliance with King David of Israel, one which would turn into a friendship (2 SAM. 5:11; 1 CHR. 14:1; 1 KGS. 5:1).[169] When Solomon succeeded his father David as king, Solomon would ask Hiram to help build the Temple in Jerusalem (2 CHR. 2). Hiram and the Phoenicians had great experience in the building and consecrating of temples, having built many to honour the pagan gods Zeus, Hercules, Melquart (son of Baal) and Astarte.[170] He was committed to the worship of these false gods and introduced them to the Israelites through his strong relationship with King Solomon.[171]

Hiram agreed to help build Solomon's Temple by providing the mighty cedars of Lebanon in its construction along with many skilled workers that the Israelites lacked (1 KGS. 5:1-18). This could be an allusion to the king we are looking for, the Assyrian, who was called a cedar of Lebanon and a cedar of the garden of God itself (EZEK. 31:3-18). The Canaanite ancestry of the Phoenicians and Assyrians was established in the study of Canaan in the second chapter (ISA. 10:5-6; 14:24-26). The Phoenician people called themselves Canaanites because the land of Canaan later became the stronghold for the Assyrians and the Phoenicians. In particular, it was the Phoenician city of Sidon or Zidon, the creation of Canaan's son of the same name. Throughout the ages, the continuing legacy of the Canaanites would become associated with the Sidonians and Tyrians. This means that Hiram's lineage can be traced back to this cursed son of Ham and the latent carrier of the Nephilim seed through the deluge. This gives further credence to the idea of Hiram as the Assyrian (ISA. 14:24-27) and the

[169] Josephus, "Against Apion," 1.106-116.

[170] Ibid.; Josephus, "Antiquities of the Jews," 8.141.

[171] Pandan, "Astarte the Goddess of Love and Beauty," *Cosmons*, October 19, 2020. https://cosmons.com/canaanite-religion/canaanite-gods-and-goddesses/astaroth-goddess-of-love-and-beauty/.

prince of Tyre (EZEK. 28:1-10) spoken of in prophecy surrounding the Antichrist.

It is this direct involvement in the building of the Temple of God, not of its destruction, that distinguishes Hiram from the other kings on this list. That is not to say Hiram did not have nefarious intentions. As purported by the Rabbis, the true purpose behind his assistance to Israel was to "sit in the seat of god." That is, to take authority of the Temple which he built. The deceptive nature of Hiram's kindness and overtures of peace are well-known in the ancient rabbinic traditions, many of which greatly precede their date of recording as oral legends. His proclivity towards self-deification is stressed repeatedly. It seems the Jews alive closer to the time of Hiram realised how he purposefully brought Solomon and the nation of Israel into idolatry and perpetual apostasy. First we read in the Babylonian Talmud that Hiram is singled out for special condemnation above the previous gentile kings:

> *I bestowed greatness upon Nimrod, and he said, Come, let us build us a city (Gen. 11:4); upon Pharaoh, and he said, who is the Lord? (Exod. 5:2) upon Sennacherib, and he said, who are they among all the gods of the countries? (2 Kgs. 18:35) upon Nebuchadnezzar and he said, I will ascend above the heights of the clouds (Isa. 14:14);* **upon Hiram King of Tyre, and he said, I will sit in the seat of god, in the heart of the seas** *(Ezek. 28:2).*[172]

The Midrashic interpretation is rather striking in its estimation of Hiram as an Antichrist figure. The many descriptions on his self-deification in opposition to the Most High standout even against the rabbinical writings on their most diabolical enemies. The seminal midrash *Genesis Rabbah* states how God "foresaw that Nebuchadnezzar and Hiram were destined to turn themselves into gods" and therefore imposed the penalty of death upon Adam and man. The passage from Ezekiel regarding the king of Tyre, whom

---

[172] B. Chullin 89a.7.

they identify as Hiram is quoted in support: "you were in Eden, the garden of God" (EZEK. 28:13) and "caused that one in Eden [Adam] to have to die."[173]

The limitless nature of Hiram's ambitions of Godhood is attested to in the later Midrashic anthology, *Yalkut Shimoni*, the most well-known and comprehensive of its kind:

> *While Hiram was floating on high the prophet Ezekiel was brought to him through the air, to reprove him for his arrogance. But the Prince of Tyre replied haughtily that he, like God, was sitting on the sea and in seven heavens, and had already survived David, Solomon, twenty-one kings of Israel, twenty kings of Judah, ten prophets, and ten high priests. Thereupon God said: "What! a mortal dares to deem himself a god because he has furnished cedars for the building of My Temple? Well, then, I will destroy My house in order that meet punishment may come upon him.*[174]

Hiram recognised the point of weakness in Solomon was his covetous heart in relation to women, wealth, and idolatry. Hiram provided great assistance to Solomon in following the inclinations of his heart in a downward path away from faithfulness to the Most High. The ancient historians Menander of Pergamus and Laetus who had access to the Tyrian archives said that Hiram gave his daughter to Solomon to cement the diplomatic ties between the two kingdoms.[175] It would be the first of many Sidonian women to be introduced into the harem of Solomon by Hiram I. In *The Historians' History of the World*, author Henry Williams recorded the historical testimony of Solomon's Sidionian harem:

---

173 Genesis Rabbah 9:5.1-3.

174 Yalkut Shimoni on Nach 367.5.

175 Clement of Alexandria, "Stromateis," 1.21.

> *That Solomon married a daughter of Hiram is reported by two authors who have written on Phœnician history, Chætus and Menander of Pergamus. Biblical history records the marriage of Solomon with the daughter of an Egyptian king, and also mentions the Jewish king's large harem, in which were also Sidonian women, for whom Solomon established the racial cult of the Sidonians, the worship of Astarte. This would indicate for the Sidonians an unusually high position in the harem.*[176]

The biblical account agrees that these foreign wives "turned away his heart after other gods" such as Astarte (Ashtoreth) of the Sidonians (Phoenicians) and Molech of the Ammonites, and influenced him to build "high places of worship" for all these false gods (1 Kgs. 11:4-8, 33; 2 Kgs. 23:13). Solomon began a process of idol worship and venerating false gods among his people, drawing them into his own rebellion. Solomon and the Israelites would have been worshipping a false Cross before Jesus died on it. The symbol of the Phoenician sun-god Astarte was the high cross, and there were even sacrificial rites of crucifixion.[177]

False Pillars in the Temple of God

The ancient historian Eusebius, in quoting Eupolemus, told of how King Solomon sent Suron (Hiram) of Tyre "the golden pillar which is dedicated in the temple of Zeus at Tyre."[178] The Hellenistic historians Menander and Dius, who had access to the Tyrian archives, recorded how Hiram adorned the temple of Jupiter (Roman equiv. of Zeus) with donations of gold, including the dedication of the golden pillar from Solomon.[179] This may be

---

[176] Williams, "The Phoenician Time of Power," in vol. 2 of The Historians' History of the World, 282-283, https://www.gutenberg.org/files/52177/52177-h/52177-h.htm.

[177] Carus, "The Cross and Its Significance," *The Open Court* 1899, no. 3 (1899): 158-159, https://opensiuc.lib.siu.edu/ocj/vol1899/iss3/2/.

[178] Eusebius, *Preparation for the Gospel*, 9.30-34 or 447-450.

[179] Josephus, "Antiquities of the Jews," 8.141; Josephus "Against Apion," 1.106.

another counterfeit of the work of Jesus, who will make his holy people pillars in the temple of God:

> *The one who is victorious I will make a pillar in the temple of my God. Never again will they leave it. I will write on them the name of my God and the name of the city of my God, the new Jerusalem, which is coming down out of heaven from my God; and I will also write on them my new name (Rev. 3:12 NKJV).*

The foundational Freemason legend of Hiram Abiff tells a similar tale of Hiram Abiff concealing the sacred name of god from all but the Master Masons. Hiram Abiff is mentioned in the Bible as being sent to Solomon by King Hiram to be the chief architect behind the Temple (1 KGS. 7:13-51; 2 CHR. 2:13-14). Hiram Abiff is said to be the son of a Tyrian man and a widowed woman of the tribe of Naphtali (1 KGS. 7:13-14; 2 CHR. 2:13-14). Notably, all who reach the Master Mason degree in Freemasonry are called "the children of the widow." This widow is said to have come from the land of Dan, the area north of Judah near the Phoenician border (1 KGS. 7:13-14; 2 CHR. 2:14). The people of the two tribes freely intermarried with the Phoenicians which effectively kept the line of David close to the Phoenician king—Hiram I. The tribe of Dan also introduced idolatry to the rest of the tribes of Israel, and God warns those who swear "by the god of Dan," the false idols, "will fall and not rise again" (AMOS 8:14).

Besides Hiram Abiff, the only other Masonic Grandmasters just so happened to be King Solomon and Hiram I. In *The Constitutions of the Free-Masons*, a historical documentation on Freemasonry all the way back from 1723,[180] author James Anderson identified them as such:

---

[180] The American founding father Benjamin Franklin would himself publish "The Constitutions of the Free-Masons" for readers in America. This was the first Masonic book printed in America.

"The wise King Solomon was Grand Master of the Lodge at Jerusalem, the learned King Hiram was Grand Master of the Lodge at Tyre, and the inspired Hiram Abiff was Master of Work."[181]

The identification of these figures as the original Grandmasters holds true to this day. The Masonic organization *Universal Co-Masonry* posits that roughly "nine out of ten" Freemasons of the present day believe that Freemasonry in its contemporary form was first devised by Solomon, "and assumed its position as a secret society" during the "construction of the Temple."[182] This would explain why Hiram and Solomon shared an interest and an aptitude for riddles and dark sayings, the hallmark of Freemasonry, and an attribute possessed by the Antichrist in abundance (DAN. 8:23).[183] The ancient historians Josephus, Dius, and Menander of Ephesus recorded that Solomon and Hiram I frequently sent each other "sophisms and enigmatical sayings" to discover "their hidden meaning."[184] Josephus said that this "philosophic inclination of theirs" cemented their friendship.[185]

Consequences of Idolatry

These acts of idolatry by the king were an abomination before God who declared that He would set His face against those who gave themselves to the detestable idol of Molech worshipped by human sacrifice (LEV. 18:21; 20:2-5). To His word, God broke up His own kingdom on earth over the wickedness of Solomon:

---

[181] Anderson, James. *The Constitutions of the Free-Masons*, 17, https://digitalcommons.unl.edu/cgi/viewcontent.cgi?article=1028&context=libraryscience.

[182] Universal Co-Masonry, "King Solomon's Temple," https://www.universalfreemasonry.org/en/history-freemasonry/king-solomon-temple.

[183] Josephus, "Antiquities of the Jews," 8.141.

[184] Ibid., Josephus also cited the ancient historical works of Dius and Menander of Ephesus who wrote on the Tyrian records, 1.106-116.

[185] Ibid., 1.106.

> *So the Lord became angry with Solomon, because his heart had turned from the Lord God of Israel, who had appeared to him twice, and had commanded him concerning this thing, that he should not go after other gods; but he did not keep what the Lord had commanded. Therefore the Lord said to Solomon, "Because you have done this, and have not kept My covenant and My statutes, which I have commanded you, I will surely tear the kingdom away from you and give it to your servant. Nevertheless I will not do it in your days, for the sake of your father David; I will tear it out of the hand of your son. However I will not tear away the whole kingdom; I will give one tribe to your son for the sake of My servant David, and for the sake of Jerusalem which I have chosen" (1 Kgs. 11:9-13 NKJV).*

After the death of Solomon, the kingdom was split between the kingdoms of Judah and Israel, and the Phoenician bloodline soon infiltrated both of them. King Ahab of Israel married Jezebel, the daughter of the Phoenician king Ithobaal I, and their daughter Athaliah married Jehoram, the king of Judah (1 Kgs. 21:20-29; 2 Kgs. 3:1-2; 8:16-19). Jehoram followed in the footsteps of Solomon by ignoring God's warnings (Mic. 6:16; 2 Chr. 21) and "caused the people of Jerusalem to prostitute themselves and [lead] Judah astray" (2 Chr. 21:11). He corrupted the Davidic kingdom by siring children with the Phoenician Athaliah—thereby integrating her condemned strain into the line of Davidic kings (2 Chr. 24:7; 2 Kgs. 8:25-26; 11:1).[186] It would be twelve generations before a king of Israel called Josiah would replace the false idols of the Phoenicians introduced by Hiram (2 Kgs. 23:1). But the biblical texts show that despite the faithfulness of Josiah in publicly pulling down the strongholds of the Phoenician cults, its influence had so pervaded the consciousness of Israel that idolatrous worship was

---

[186] Watch Tower Bible and Tract Society, "Genealogy of Jesus Christ," in *Insight on the Scriptures* 1, 915.

quickly reinstated in the kingdom (2 KGS. 23:24-27).[187] Exile was inevitable. The late Messianic believer Art Katz noted how the perpetuity of their apostasy and backsliding is "ever ongoing" until the end of the age (JER. 8:44-45).[188] Hiram introduced a terminal strain of ungodliness into the national consciousness of Israel, and it would take a divine redeemer in Christ to restore them to godliness (ROM. 11:26-27; PSA. 14:7; ISA. 59:20-21).

As we discussed in the first chapter, the Amalekites from Esau are inextricably linked to the Phoenicians. It was Solomon's responsibility to destroy Amalek before building the Temple but he promoted the spirit of Amalek instead through the Phoenician Hiram I. This grave act of disobedience allows Amalek to arise once again at the end of the age, spiritually animated by Satan himself (ISA. 14:12-20; EZEK. 28:12-19). If a man of the stature and wisdom of Solomon can slide from an exalted place to a thoroughly deceived position so very easily, then how needful for us to be continually on our guard against the wiles of an enemy of angelic brilliance. A leader of Israel in the character of Solomon (False Prophet) along with the help of Hiram shall again rebuild the Temple but divert worship away from Yahweh. It will be a new Tower of Babel as built by Nimrod the prototype, a symbol of cosmic opposition to the true God above in heaven.

The Hiram-Solomon 666 Connection

According to the encyclopedia *The Historians' History of the World,* Jewish historiography "does not conceal the fact that the external brilliancy and wealth of Solomon were a consequence of the connection with the rich and artistic neighbouring nation [Hiram and Phoenicia]."[189] As biblical evidence, we can consult

---

[187] Fuller Seminary, "Josiah's Reform." Fuller Seminary," https://www.fuller.edu/next-faithful-step/resources/josiahs-reform/.

[188] Katz, "Redemptions and Creation," *Sermon Index,* March 28, 2009, video, 1:11:17, https://youtu.be/VoIAgkBGmoo.

[189] Williams, "The Phoenician Time of Power," in vol. 2 of *The Historians' History of the World,* 282-283, https://www.gutenberg.org/files/52177/52177-h/52177-h.htm.

both 2 Chronicles 9 and 1 Kings 10 which tell of Solomon's splendour as the fruits of the strong economic alliance with Hiram. "The weight of the gold that Solomon received yearly was 666 talents" from trade (2 CHR. 9:13; 1 KGS. 10:14). Solomon's fleet of trading ships is said to be "manned by Hiram's servants," who would return to Solomon with the gold and other treasures (2 CHR. 9:21; 1 KGS. 10:22). The mention of 666, the number of the beast is peculiar. The weight of gold is said to exclude the revenues from the merchants, traders, the kings of Arabia, and the governors of the country (1 KGS. 10:15). The exclusion of all of these sources of gold seems arbitrary unless the total of 666 talents of gold is used symbolically here. As it would happen, the only other explicit references to 666 in scripture relate to Adonikam (EZRA 2:13) and the beast (REV. 13:18). The first of these scriptures will soon be discussed, while the other is clear in its allusion to the Antichrist. In the case of Solomon, it seems to me that this great personal accumulation of wealth totalling 666 indicates that the source was merely material. It came from the coffers of Phoenicia, and it came at a price. It was not sanctioned by God for the wealth of the nation, but by Hiram for its subversion. That "King Solomon was greater in riches and wisdom than all the other kings of the earth" was not for the glorification of God who endowed him with this wisdom. I believe the wisdom of Solomon had regressed to an earthly wisdom under the influence of King Hiram. Consider the following scripture:

> *So the Lord gave Solomon wisdom, as He had promised*
> *him; and there was peace between Hiram and Solomon,*
> *and the two of them made a treaty together (1 Kgs. 5:12*
> *NKJV).*

This suggests the peace that came from their treaty or pact was connected to this wisdom. Solomon's father David had already enjoyed a peaceful relationship with Hiram, so what were the terms? Did this involve Solomon's perversion of the wisdom from God into the earthly wisdom of the mystery religions to which they were essentially united in heart and mind?

Another interesting but speculative reference to 666 in relation to Hiram and Solomon lies in the Hebrew gematria of "Hiram Solomon." Again, this is only used in support of the biblical connection between Hiram and Solomon as 666. While the total does not equal 666, but 633, the remainder of 33 is a significant piece of the puzzle because of its connection to the fallen angels. One third (33%) of the angels are said to have fallen into rebellion (REV. 12:4); the latitude of Mount Hermon, the mountain the fallen angels descended upon is 33°; there are 33° in Freemasonry, the bastion for the spiritual offspring of the fallen angels; and in the occult at large, the number 33 represents the higher consciousness of the Luciferic light.

Hiram and Solomon, Mimics of Antichrist and False Prophet?

From our studies so far, the relationship between Hiram and Solomon seems to resemble that of the Antichrist and False Prophet to each other and to Israel itself. The beast (Antichrist) comes from the sea, the symbol for gentile humanity (REV. 13:1-10) and is supported by the second beast (False Prophet) which comes from the earth, the symbol for the land of Israel (REV. 13:11-18). This matches Hiram and Solomon. The Antichrist is revealed to be a gentile with the support of a Jewish False Prophet, possibly from the tribe of Dan, the tribe which God is to judge for leading Israel into idolatry (1 KGS. 12:25-33; 14:7-16; 2 KGS. 10:29; AMOS 8:14; GEN. 49:17; REV. 7:4-8). This is significant because the Antichrist and the False Prophet are inextricably connected, and so were Hiram and Solomon. The Antichrist cannot be fully understood without unpacking his symbiotic relationship with the second beast, the False Prophet. They are intertwined in a counterfeit union duplicating the interrelationship between Jesus and the Holy Spirit. Just as Jesus cannot be fully known except for the witness and revelation of the Holy Spirit, and conversely the Holy Spirit cannot be fully known and experienced without going through the "door" which is Jesus (JOHN 10:7-16).[190] Their union is a pivotal part of the concluding drama of this present evil age where they will seek to rise to total dominance with the help of the third member of their trinity, Satan.

Going Forward with the Antichrist Assumption

If we assume for a moment that Hiram is indeed the first incarnation of the Antichrist, the very antithesis of Christ, the following passage from 1 Kings may contain significant subtext:

> *King Solomon gave twenty towns in Galilee to Hiram king of Tyre, because Hiram had supplied him with all the cedar and juniper and gold he wanted. But when Hiram went from Tyre to see the towns that Solomon had given him, he was not pleased with them. "What kind of towns are these you have given me, my brother?" he asked. And he called them the Land of Kabul, a name they have to this day (1 Kgs. 9:11-13 NIV).*

The Phoenician meaning of Kabul denotes "what does not please" or "good for nothing."[191] Hiram was given Galilee, including its most despised town, Nazareth, of which it was said nothing good could come out of it (JOHN 1:46). It is fair to say they were not the most esteemed of lands, but it was not for Solomon to give in the first place. God had allocated them to the Israelites under the kingdom of God. It is telling that Jesus, who was of Nazareth, did not despise its stature despite being esteemed above all men. No, he walked among the meek and downtrodden who dwelled there. For Hiram who had once received these lands as a gift, still he expressed his great displeasure of it. The rationale behind this attitude seemed strange to me, but what is stranger is the very inclusion of the verse. Perhaps there is greater subtext behind it

---

[190] Gelderen, "Honoring the Holy Spirit as God," *Revival Focus*, https://www.revivalfocus.org/honoring-holy-spirit-god/.

[191] Ibid.

that alludes to the mindset of Lucifer as he worked through Hiram. We know Hiram was instrumental in constructing the Temple, and that Lucifer intends on taking his seat upon its throne, so when Solomon presented Hiram with the lands of Galilee, implicit was the reminder of where the true King and High Priest was truly from. While the eighth king may take his seat upon the throne of the Temple, it is ultimately the son of the woman to whom it bears witness that will reign supreme for all time. While Lucifer is yet to accomplish this goal, and may have actually attempted this through Hiram, you can be assured that he will when he re-emerges and brokers peace in the Middle East with the rebuilding of the Temple as a condition.

Hiram as the Beast who ascends out of the Abyss

The beast that is yet to ascend out of the abyss, the bottomless pit (REV. 9:1; 11:7; 17:8-11), will express the characteristics of the seven kings, and it is my own contention that the beast will be the eighth king, the Antichrist. That for John the beast had been, was not, and yet will be, indicates to me a reincarnation of one of the first five who had fallen in John's day. With this in mind, I will share the ancient legend of the phoenix as a parallel of this beast prophecy. The common detail among the many recontextualizations of the legend is of a dying and rising phoenix bird. It destroys itself in flames and rises from its own ashes in a cycle of regeneration or rebirth. In the book *Masonic & Occult Symbols Illustrated* the author Cathy Burns makes an interesting observation:

> *Most occultists believe that the Phoenix is a symbol of Lucifer who was cast down in flames and who (they think) will one day rise triumphant. This, of course, also relates to the rising of Hiram Abiff, the Masonic Christ.*[192]

---

[192] Burns, *Masonic and Occult Symbols Illustrated*, 121-123.

The link between the Phoenix and the Phoenicians is striking. The word *Phoenix* and *Phoenicia* appear to be from the same root. In Greek mythology, the son of Agenor the king of Tyre was called *Phoenix*, and was the eponym of Phoenicia. He was also the brother or father of Europa (Europe) depending on the source. Religious scholar Roel van den Broek thinks *phoenix* could mean 'the Phoenician bird' or 'the purplish-red bird,' the colour of their greatest dye export.[193] With all of this in mind, perhaps the image of a dying and rising Phoenician portrays the rebirth of Hiram I and his rise from the bottomless pit? Let us continue with this line of thought.

You may remember our discussion about the Masonic legend surrounding Hiram Abiff and Tubal-Cain. Hiram Abiff is pulled through the molten sea into the centre of the earth of fire, and is handed a hammer to restore order from chaos. Tubal-Cain blesses Hiram to re-ascend to earth and begat a son to restore "order out of chaos" by defeating the sons of Adam, the seed in opposition to the seed of Cain. We see the same imagery of a consuming death by fire and a rebirth or ascension from the ashes. Was the centre of the earth of fire a symbolic picture of the abyss, and the son a picture of the promised seed of the serpent who ascends from there and offers man a way out of chaos and back to order?

Hiram the Rising Phoenician-Phoenix

I am going to propose a speculative connection between Hiram and the dying and rising from the abyss prophecy. To do so, I need to introduce two additional characters which pair with Hiram to produce a peculiar message. I will first note that Hiram was also called Adonhiram or Adoniram meaning *Lord Hiram*. The first character is *Adonikam*, a name similar to Adoniram, who is recorded in Ezra as returning from the Babylonian captivity (parallel to the captivity of the fallen angels in the abyss) with 666 descendants (EZRA 2:13). As previously stated, this was the only

[193] Van den Broek, *The Myth of the Phoenix*, 62-66.

direct reference to 666 in the Bible that is not tied to Solomon-Hiram or the beast. Interestingly, in the same list of returning exiles from Nehemiah, Adonikam is instead called Adonijah (NEH. 10:16), whose namesake happens to match a son of King David who conspired to take his throne (1 KGS. 1). This is significant because the throne of David is destined for Jesus to reinstate after the final judgement (REV. 22:16; LUKE 1:32-33; PSA. 110; MATT. 2:1-6; 22:41-46; MARK 12:35-37; ISA. 9:6-7; 11:1; 42:1-9; 49:7; JER. 23:5-6; 33:14-17). Jesus is repeatedly depicted as the one greater than David, and David himself referred to Jesus as his lord at the right hand of the Lord (PSA. 110). This seems to foreshadow the Luciferic challenge to the Davidic throne by his son, the Antichrist, in the character of Adonijah, who rises out of the abyss like the beast.

After the conspiracy failed, Adonijah fled and took refuge at an altar. Solomon graciously pardoned him for his conduct on the condition that he showed himself "a worthy man" (1 KGS. 1:5-53). Adonijah would later mount a second attempt to steal the throne but was seized and put to death (1 KGS. 2:13-25). By this same token, Lucifer mounted a rebellion in heaven seeking the throne of the son of God and was granted an opportunity for repentance in the garden of Eden. Lucifer established his altar in the tree of the knowledge of good and evil and willingly rejected his chance of reconciliation with God. Instead, he recruited Adam and Eve, and thus man, into his rebellion to mount a second and final offensive against the Most High. Jesus, like Solomon, prevented Lucifer from taking the throne of David intended for him and his godly line at the cross. When Lucifer tries a second time in the person of the Antichrist in parallel to Adonijah, Jesus will cast him into the Lake of Fire (REV. 19:20; 20:10).

With this background out of the way, I propose that these three men paint a composite picture of a man soon to reappear on the world stage who came from the abyss:

Image 5.4 – Hebrew meanings for the names Adonhiram, Adonijah and Adonikam which present an interesting message.

NAME	MEANING
Adonhiram	Lord Hiram
Adonijah	Lord Yahweh
Adonikam	Lord Rising

We can interpret this two-fold. Firstly, I believe the meaning of these three names from the ungodly perspective works as "Hiram is Yahweh Rising." Linking the meanings to the characters behind the names, we could restate this as "Hiram desires to rise to Yahweh's place from out of his captivity in the abyss." Secondly, Lucifer seeks to rise as lord of the ungodly line either in the character of Hiram, or *as Hiram*, to ascend to the greatness of Yahweh. We can take this as meaning Lucifer and Yahweh, lords of their respective lines, are to rise in the end days to fight for supremacy over the other.

Image 5.5 – The gematria values behind phrases associating Hiram with the messianic roles of king and high priest.

WORD(S)	GEMATRIA VALUE
Hiram King of Tyre + Yahweh	666 (638 + 28)
King Hiram Canaanite High Priest	666

Here we read that Hiram longs to take the place of Yahweh as king and high priest. The Messiah to come was expected to be both king and priest. As we know, Jesus has assumed both of these titles, and the Antichrist will attempt the same. He will try to steal the ark of the covenant for his own possession like the Philistines did (1 SAM. 4:1-11). This being the coveted place of Jesus the true Messiah for himself. We know from Revelation 11 that from the sounding of the seventh trumpet when God in Christ prepares to execute judgement, the ark is secure in the Temple of heaven (REV. 11:15-19). The movements of the Antichrist are doomed to fail, and he shall be sent to the place of everlasting perdition, a destination fitting for one called the son of perdition (2 THESS. 2:3-4; REV. 19:20-21).

The Seven Kings

In this chapter we have simultaneously presented two possible interpretations of the seven kings prophecy of Revelation 17 (REV. 17:9-11). I provided my reasoning for why I believe the seven kings are literal kings, but I still ordered the candidates by the time of their respective kingdoms. In this interpretation, the reconstituted Roman Empire would be the seventh head (kingdom) for the eighth king.

The Eighth King as a Symbiosis of the Seven

The first possibility we have explored is that the eighth king, the beast (Antichrist), is a symbiosis of the seven kings in character and conduct. That he exhibits all of their adversarial qualities and commits all of the same atrocities against the holy people, but on a greater magnitude. I have produced a table and description below that shows these seven kings ordered by kingdom and their significance to the eighth king:

Image 5.6 – The final seven king candidates for the Revelation 17 prophecy.

KING AND KINGDOM	SIGNIFICANCE TO THE EIGHTH KING
Pharaoh (Egypt)	Resists Israelite deliverance and suffers plagues
Hiram I (Phoenicia-Assyria)	Builds the third temple for Satan
Nimrod (Babylon)	Consolidates power in a world government
Cyrus (Medo-Persia)	Brokers Middle East peace deal
Antiochus Epiphanes (Greece)	Abomination of desolation in the Temple
Hadrian (Rome)	Deports the Jews from Israel
Hitler (Germany-Holy Roman Empire)	Attempts to exterminate the Jews

Combined Characteristics of the Seven Kings

The Antichrist will blaspheme God by saying "who is the Lord that I should fear him?" (Pharaoh) as he takes for himself the seat of God in the rebuilt Temple (Hiram I). Emboldened by his control of a centralised world government (Nimrod) enabled by a successful peace deal in the Middle East (Cyrus), he will attack the God of Israel and the saints. In the Temple he will recapitulate the abomination of desolation (Antiochus) and the Jews and Christians who heed the warnings of Jesus will begin to disperse from the promised land (Hadrian). This marks the period of great persecution and genocide of the Jews and those who protect them (Hitler). The final stage of the concluding drama will be set and judgement by God is all that will follow.

The Eighth King as One of the Seven

In the second case, the eighth king is literally one of the seven. That is, the human incarnation of Satan that has been here before in the personage of one of these seven kings. This means he will return as the eighth king also being one of the seven. Just as Jesus will have his second coming, so will Satan.

If we assume this literal interpretation, in light of all the evidence presented, Hiram I would be my top suspect for the eighth king, the human vessel of Lucifer. Jews today would readily accept a gentile leader in the character of Hiram I who comes with overtures of peace and offers to help rebuild the Temple. I believe he is the only one of the seven kings who could return and find widespread acceptance from Jews or gentiles with any measure of trust. Cyrus could certainly find equal favour but lacks the diabolical qualities to be the man of sin and lawlessness.

I personally believe Hiram recognised the pre-eminence of the God of Israel but out of pride sought to rise above God inside His Temple (EZEK. 28:2; ISA. 14:13). His strategy was victory through deception in parallel to the Antiochene Antichrist prophesied by Daniel (DAN. 8:23-25; 11:21-23). I believe he awaits his second advent to be able to fully express the composite character shown through all the kings of the serpent line. Nebuchadnezzar repented of his grandiose ideas of being a god (DAN. 4:34-37), but not so concerning Hiram, King of Tyre.

If Hiram is indeed the eighth king, he could be joined with the second beast, the False Prophet to build the Third Temple. The False Prophet shall be a leader of Israel in the character of King Solomon of Israel who is animated by the same Luciferic spirit. He will devote himself to the cause of the beast, Hiram King of Tyre.

Conclusion

We are steadily moving towards a final irreversible conflict between two incompatible spiritual forces. The God of creation is defending Himself in righteousness from the false gods who have deemed themselves worthy of replacing Him despite owing their existence to Him. I stated in the introduction that all of mankind are in the process of giving allegiance to one side or the other— whether they are aware of it or not. It is basically an inner inclination of the heart which the mind comes into agreement with. The spirit of the age is constantly directing our minds to a spiritual domain not authorised by our Creator but permitted out of respect for our free will. God allows us to follow our heart, the mantra of the age, even if it is devoted to the ungodly domain opened to us through the tree of the knowledge of good and evil. By repentance and faith in the Word of God alone, we can be guided out of Lucifer's mighty deception, and live forever restored in God's presence. Failing this, either by rejecting God until your end, or through union with the beast by receiving his mark, the prospect of this eternal union will be no more. And of course, you may be more than satisfied with that outcome, and possibly be inclined to support the goal of usurping Jesus from his esteemed place of exaltation and worship. It is up to each individual to decide for themselves which tree represents wisdom and enlightenment. Here are some questions to ponder for the undecided:

- Which son of the Father will I give myself over to in mind, heart, and soul?

- Was the serpent correct in promising we shall be as gods, or was the Lord correct in claiming we are sons of God who are dependent on him?

- Is faithfulness to the tree of life too narrow and limiting or is it the true source of ultimate goodness?

- Did the serpent (Lucifer) from the garden of Eden liberate mankind by tempting Adam and Eve into eating from the tree of the knowledge of good and evil?

- Is self-exaltation possible or desirable independent of God, or is giving glory to God our true purpose?

May you choose well. Eternity is before you and when the final curtain on your life comes down your destiny is confirmed and sealed. I sincerely hope this book has helped you on your spiritual journey, whether you are reading as a Christian, as a follower of another faith, or as an atheist.

Where to go from here

The question left to consider is whether Jesus of Nazareth is the seed of the woman. Throughout this book we have operated under the assumption that he is, but in our companion book "Seed of God: Jesus Christ" we will qualify this assumption. A wide range of evidence or watermarks that are carefully embedded into the Old and New Testaments will support the divinity of Jesus. If Jesus Christ is the human manifestation of God, the seed of the woman, it must be Jesus who is to execute the final blow to the serpent's head and end the transgression. This of course, necessitates him being all that the New Testament claims he is in light of Old Testament revelation.

I greatly encourage you to avail yourself of this book, whether you are a firm believer in Jesus as the Messiah or not. After all, a rational faith is built upon the initial foundation of evidence and strengthened thereafter with the deeper spiritual faith. The rational evidence can also lift your spiritual convictions and bring you closer to God. Ultimately, the choice is in your hands, so I hope you consider taking the time to look over our perspective presented on the godly side, and our contention that he is its true federal head in "Seed of God: Jesus Christ."

If you enjoyed this book, please consider leaving a rating or a review on Amazon at the store page "Seed of Satan: Antichrist."

I have also published a companion to this book called "Seed of God: Jesus Christ" and written free articles on the website beholdmessiah.com which further explore these topics.

References

Ahern, Kevin. "Pope Francis Calls for a Stronger System of Global Governance." *America*, September 25, 2015. https://papalvisit.americamedia.org/2015/09/25/pope-francis-calls-for-a-stronger-system-of-global-governance/.

Akin, Danny. "Antiochus Epiphanes and Antichrist: The Arch Enemies of God's People – Daniel 11:21-45." *Danny Akin*, January 19, 2017. http://www.danielakin.com/wp-content/uploads/2017/01/Daniel-11.21-45-Antiochus-Epiphanes-and-Antichrist.-The-Arch-Enemies-of-Gods-People-manuscript-kh.pdf.

Anderson, James. *The Constitutions of the Free-Masons*. Philadelphia: Benjamin Franklin, 1734. https://digitalcommons.unl.edu/cgi/viewcontent.cgi?article=1028&context=libraryscience.

Bailey, Alice. *Education in the New Age*. New York: Lucis Publishing Co., 1954.

———. *Esoteric Psychology*. Vol. 2, New York: Lucis Publishing Co., 1960.

———. *The Externalisation of the Hierarchy*. New York: Lucis Publishing Co., 1957.

———. "The Fourteen Rules for Group Initiation." *In The Rays and Initiations,* rule 13. Vol. 5 of *A Treatise on the Seven Rays*. New York: Lucis Publishing Co., 1960.

Barclay, William. *The Revelation of John*. London: The Westminster Press, 1960.

BBC. "Archbishop Becomes Druid." *BBC*, August 5, 2002. http://news.bbc.co.uk/2/hi/uk_news/wales/2172918.stm.

Black, John. "The Powerful Symbol of the Swastika and its 12,000 Year History." *Ancient Origins*, April 1, 2019. https://www.ancient-origins.net/myths-legends/symbol-swastika-and-its-12000-year-old-history-001312.

Bostrom, Nick. "A History of Transhumanist Thought." *Journal of Evolution and Technology* 14, no. 1 (April 2005): 1-25.

Brockmann, Stephen. *Nuremberg: The Imaginary Capital*. Rochester: Camden House, 2006.

Brzozowski, Alexandra. "Macron Seeks Revival of Weimar Triangle, Defence Ties During Warsaw Visit." *EURACTIV*, February 4, 2020. https://www.euractiv.com/section/future-eu/news/macron-seeks-revival-of-weimar-triangle-defence-ties-during-warsaw-visit/.

Bundy, Joel. "Allegories of Hiram Abiff: Exoteric and esoteric philosophies from Christianity, Rosicrucianism, and the ancient Egyptian mystery schools." *Virginia Royal Arch Research Chapter no. 1753*, July 16, 2016. https://virginiaroyalarch.org/education/pdfs/Allegories_of_Hiram_Abiff.pdf.

Burns, Cathy. *Masonic and Occult Symbols Illustrated*. Sharing, 1998.

Carpenter, Ron. "Why Did Jesus Go to Caesarea Philippi?" *A Carpenter's View*, February 20, 2019. https://teachingforsotzambia.com/2019/02/20/1040/.

Carr, Harry. *The Freemason at Work*. Oxfordshire: Burgess & Son, 1976.

Carus, Paul. "The Cross and Its Significance. With Illustrations of Assyrian, Egyptian Jewish, Phoenician, Indian, Tibetan, Grecian, Roman, Teutonic and Oceanic Crosses." *The Open Court* 1899, no. 3 (1899): 158-159. https://opensiuc.lib.siu.edu/ocj/vol1899/iss3/2/.

Chossudovsky, Michel. "The Ultimate Weapon of Mass Destruction: 'Owning the Weather' for Military Use." *Global Research*, July 5, 2018. https://www.globalresearch.ca/the-ultimate-weapon-of-mass-destruction-owning-the-weather-for-military-use-2/5306386.

Cicero, Marcus Tullius. "For Lucius Murena." Translated by C. D. Yonge. In *The Orations of Marcus Tullius Cicero*. London: Henry G. Bohn, 1856.

———. *On Divination*. Translated by William Armistead Falconer. Cambridge: Harvard University Press, 1923.

Clausen, Henry C. *Emergence of the Mystical*. San Diego: Neyenesch Printers, 1980.

Cloud, David. "Hadrian: The Enemy of God." *Way of Life Literature*, September 12, 2018. https://www.wayoflife.org/reports/hadrian_the_enemy_of_god.php.

Creme, Benjamin. *The Reappearance of the Christ and the Masters of Wisdom*. 2nd ed. Berkeley: Share International Foundation, 2007.

Dawkins, Richard. Interview by Ben Stein, *Expelled: No Intelligence Allowed*, April 18, 2008. Video, 2:01. https://youtu.be/BoncJBrrdQ8.

Delio, Ilia. "Teilhard De Chardin and The Future of God." *Center for Christogenesis*, September 5, 2016. https://christogenesis.org/teilhard-de-chardin-and-the-future-of-god/.

Delitzsch, Franz, and Carl Friedrich Keil. *Biblical Commentary on the Old Testament*. Edinburgh: T. & T. Clark, 1857.

Dennis, Rabbi Geoffrey W. "What Is Kabbalah?" *Reform Judaism*. https://reformjudaism.org/beliefs-practices/spirituality/what-kabbalah.

Derek Prince. "Where Are We In Biblical Prophecy, Pt 5 - Will The Antichrist Arise In Europe?" June 12, 2015. Video, 1:43:20. https://youtu.be/OvKQWvDRiaA.

Dio, Cassius. "Roman History, Volume I: Books 1-11." Translated by Earnest Cary, Herbert B. Foster. In *Loeb Classical Library* 32. Cambridge: Harvard University Press, 1914.

Diprose, Ronald E. *Israel and the Church: The Origins and Effects of Replacement Theology*. Milton Keynes: Authentic Media, 2004.

Duncan, Malcolm. *Duncan's Masonic Ritual and Monitor*. New York City: Dick & Fitzgerald, 1866.

Drews, Robert. "Canaanites and Philistines." *Journal for the Study of the Old Testament* 23, no. 81 (December 1998): 39–61. https://doi.org/10.1177/030908929802308104.

Eusebius of Caesarea. "Church History." Translated by Arthur McGiffert. In *Nicene and Post-Nicene Fathers, Second Series* 1. Buffalo: Christian Literature Publishing Co., 1890.

———. *Preparation for the Gospel.* Translated by E. H. Gifford. Oxford: University Press, 1903.

Fessier, Bruce. "Annunaki, Nephilim and Denisovans? Contact in Desert Explores Ancient Giants." *Desert Sun*, May 23, 2019. https://www.desertsun.com/story/life/entertainment/people/bruce fessierentertainment/2019/05/23/annunaki-nephilim-and-denisovans-contact-desert-explores-ancient-giants/3700717002/.

Fillard, Jean-pierre. *Is Man To Survive Science?* Singapore: World Scientific Publishing Co, 2015.

Fuller Seminary. "Josiah's Reform." *Fuller Seminary.* https://www.fuller.edu/next-faithful-step/resources/josiahs-reform/.

Gelderen, John Van. "Honoring the Holy Spirit as God." *Revival Focus,* June 6, 2017. https://www.revivalfocus.org/honoring-holy-spirit-god/.

Gerson, Michael. "Humans reach for godhood — and leave their humanity behind." *Washington Post*, June 26, 2017. https://www.washingtonpost.com/opinions/humans-reach-for-godhood—and-leave-their-humanity-behind/2017/06/26/5f74b20c-5a93-11e7-9fc6-c7ef4bc58d13_story.html.

Goebbels, Joseph. The Goebbels Diaries 1939-41. Translated by Fred Taylor. London: Hamish Hamilton Ltd, 1982.

Guiley, Rosemary. "Kabbalah." In *The Encyclopedia of Witches, Witchcraft and Wicca*, 190-91. New York: Infobase Publishing, 1989.

Hall, Manly P. *Lectures on Ancient Philosophy.* New York: TarcherPerigee, 1929.

———. *The Secret Teachings of All Ages*. New York: TarcherPerigee, 1928.

———. *What the Ancient Wisdom Expects of Its Disciples*. Los Angeles: Philosophical Research Society, 1925.

Hamp, Douglas. "Adam's Biophotons and Future Bodies of Light." Chap. 2 in *Corrupting the Image: Angels, Aliens, and the Antichrist Revealed*. Scotts Valley: CreateSpace, 2011.

Harari, Yuval Noah. *Homo Deus: A History of Tomorrow*. New York: Harper, 2017.

Hassler, Mark A. "The Identity of the Little Horn in Daniel 8: Antiochus IV Epiphanes, Rome, or The Antichrist?" *Master's Seminary Journal* 27, no. 1 (Spring 2016): 33-44.

Henderson, Bernard W. *The Life and Principate of the Emperor Hadrian*. New York: Brentano's Publishers, 1916.

Herodotus. *Histories*. Translated by A. D. Godley. Cambridge: Harvard University Press, 1920.

Horace. "Odes." Translated by John Conington. In *The Odes and Carmen Saeculare of Horace*. London: George Bell and Sons, 1882.

Hume, Tim. "World's Longest Tunnel Opens Deep beneath Swiss Alps." *CNN*, June 1, 2016. https://edition.cnn.com/2016/06/01/europe/switzerland-longest-tunnel-gotthard/index.html.

IISD. *Youth Sourcebook on Sustainable Development*. Winnipeg: IISD, 1995. http://iisd.ca/youth/ysbk000.htm.

Isbouts, Jean-pierre. "Who was the Egyptian pharoah challenged Moses?" *National Geographic*, December 28, 2018. https://www.nationalgeographic.com/culture/people-in-the-bible/pharaoh-king-punished-god/.

Jerome, Saint. *Commentary on Isaiah: Origen Homilies 1-9 on Isaiah*. New York: Newman Press, 2015.

Jewish Voice. "Update on the Building of the Third Temple." *Jewish Voice*. https://www.jewishvoice.org/read/article/update-building-third-temple.

Jha, Alok. "Pope's astronomer says he would baptise an alien if it asked him." *The Guardian*, September 17, 2010.
https://www.theguardian.com/science/2010/sep/17/pope-astronomer-baptise-aliens.

Josephus, Flavius. *The Works of Flavius Josephus*. Translated by William Whiston. Auburn and Buffalo: John E. Beardsley, 1895.

Katz, Art. "Redemptions and Creation." *Sermon Index*, March 28, 2009. Video, 1:11:17. https://youtu.be/VoIAgkBGm00.

Kelchner, John Wesley. *The Bible and King Solomon's Temple in Masonry*. A.J. Holman Company, 1940.

Khorenatsi, Movses. *History of the Armenians*. Translated by Robert W. Thomson. Cambridge: Harvard University Press, 1978.

Kotkin, Stephen. "Russia's Perpetual Geopolitics: Putin Returns to the Historical Pattern." *Foreign Affairs* 95, no. 3 (2016): 2-9.
http://www.jstor.org/stable/43946851.

Lee, Witness. *The Economy of God*. 6th ed. Anaheim: Living Stream Ministry, 1968.

Lesses, Rebecca. "'They Revealed Secrets to Their Wives': The Transmission of Magical Knowledge in 1 Enoch." *With Letters of Light: Studies in the Dead Sea Scrolls, Early Jewish Apocalypticism, Magic, and Mysticism in Honor of Rachel Elior*. Berlin: Walter de Gruyter, 2011: 196-222.
https://www.marquette.edu/maqom/letters123.pdf#page=205.

Lewis, C.S. *Mere Christianity*. New York City: HarperCollins, 1952.

Mack, John E. *Abduction: Human Encounters with Aliens*. New York: Scribner, 2007.

Mackey, Albert G. *Encyclopedia of Freemasonry*. New York: The Masonic History Company, 1920.

Martyr, Justin. "First Apology." Translated by Marcus Dods and George Reith. In *Ante-Nicene Fathers* 1. Buffalo: Christian Literature Publishing Co., 1885.

McClintock, John, and James Strong. "North." In *Cyclopedia of Biblical, Theological and Ecclesiastical Literature*. New York City: Harper, 1867.

McCoy, Daniel. "Odin." Norse Mythology for Smart People. https://norse-mythology.org/gods-and-creatures/the-aesir-gods-and-goddesses/odin/.

Miller, Steven R. *Daniel*. Vol. 18 of *New American Commentary*. Nashville: Broadman & Holman, 1994.

Mizrahi, Maurice. "Why the Red Heifer?" *Congregation Adat Reyim*, July 1, 2017. https://www.adatreyim.org/divrei-torah.html.

Muller, Robert. *My Testament to the UN*. 2nd ed. New York: World Happiness & Cooperation, 1994.

Nevins, Rabbi Danny. "Noah 5775: Species Purity and the Great flood." *Rabbi Danny Nevins*. https://rabbinevins.com/2014/10/22/noah-5775-species-purity-and-the-great-flood/.

Oliver, George. The Historical Landmarks and Other Evidences of Freemasonry, Explained. *London: Richard Spencer, 1846*.

Overy, Richard. *The Dictators: Hitler's Germany, Stalin's Russia*. London: Penguin, 2004.

Pandan, Deomar. "Astarte the Goddess of Love and Beauty." *Cosmons*, October 19, 2020. https://cosmons.com/canaanite-religion/canaanite-gods-and-goddesses/astaroth-goddess-of-love-and-beauty/.

Peacock, Arlen. "The Realm of Glory: The Harlot and the Church." *Garden Place Ministries*, 2006. http://myplace.frontier.com/~arlenpeacock/harlotandthechurch.html.

Peters, Ted. "Astrotheology and the ETI Myth." *Theology and Science* 7, no. 1 (January 2009): 4.

Philostratus, Flavius. *On Heroes*. Translated by Ellen Bradshaw Aitken and Jennifer K. Berenson Maclean. Atlanta: Society of Biblical Literature, 2002.

Pike, Albert. *Morals and Dogma of the Ancient and Accepted Scottish Rite of Freemasonry*. Richmond: L. H. Jenkins, Inc. Edition Book Manufacturers, 1871.

Pliny the Elder. *Natural History*. Translated by John Bostock and H.T. Riley. London: Taylor and Francis, 1855.

Pope Francis. *Fratelli tutti*. Encyclical Letter. Vatican website. October 3, 2020. http://www.vatican.va/content/francesco/en/encyclicals/document s/papa-francesco_20201003_enciclica-fratelli-tutti.html.

Prasch, Jacob. "Nephilim, Pan and Pontifex Maximus." *Moriel TV*, July 31, 2017. Video, 53:49. https://youtu.be/Vieoe6hoUEE.

Prince, Derek. "And Then the End Shall Come, Pt 2: The Spine of Prophetic Revelation." *Derek Prince*, December 6, 2012. Video, 58:02. https://youtu.be/SX7EKSMvhkA.

Ronayne, Edmond. The Master's Carpet or Masonry and Baal-Worship Identical. *Chicago: T. B. Arnold, 1887.*

Ronen, Tsafrir. "Hadrian's Curse." *Christian Friends of Israeli Communities.* https://cfoic.com/hadrians-curse/.

Routledge, Clay. "Atheists Love Aliens." *Psychology Today*, May 2015. https://www.psychologytoday.com/blog/more-mortal/201504/atheists-love-aliens.

Shea, William. "The Antediluvians." *Geoscience Research Institute* 18, no. 1. (1991). https://www.grisda.org/origins-18010.

Shirer, William L. *Rise and Fall of the Third Reich: A History of Nazi Germany*. New York City: Simon and Schuster, 1990.

Silow-Carroll, Andrew. "Who is King Cyrus, and why did Netanyahu compare him to Trump?" *Times of Israel*, March 8, 2018. https://www.timesofisrael.com/who-is-king-cyrus-and-why-is-netanyahu-comparing-him-to-trump/.

Solinus, Gaius Julius. *Polyhistor*. Translated by Arwen Apps. Sydney: Macquarie University, 2011. https://topostext.org/work/747.

Steiner, Rudolf. "The Temple Legend: Freemasonry and Related Occult

Movements." 2nd ed. Rudolf Steiner Press, 1997.

Stradner, Ivana, and Max Frost. "NATO Has a New Weak Link for Russia to Exploit." *Foreign Policy*, April 22, 2020. https://foreignpolicy.com/2020/04/22/north-macedonia-nato-russia/.

Stuckenbruck, Loren T. "The "Angels" and "Giants" of Genesis 6:1-4 in Second and Third Century BCE Jewish Interpretation: Reflections on the Posture of Early Apocalyptic Traditions." *Dead Sea Discoveries* 7, no. 3 (2000): 354-77. http://www.jstor.org/stable/4193170.

Sumner, Paul. "Our Lady of Fatima, UFOs, and September 1994." (1994). Accessed July 12, 2020. http://www.hebrew-streams.org/works/hayom/fatima-ufo-rapture.pdf.

Tanzella-Nitti, Giuseppe. "Extraterrestrial life." *Interdisciplinary Documentation on Religion and Science*, 2008. http://inters.org/extraterrestrial-life.

Tezyapar, Sinem. "New Muslim vision for Temple Mount." *Ynetnews*, December 3, 2013. https://www.ynetnews.com/articles/0,7340,L-4355421,00.html.

Tickle, Jonny. "Russian Population to Fall by 1.2 Million by 2024." *RT*, October 16, 2020. https://www.rt.com/russia/503730-russia-population-estimate-dropping/.

Tverberg, Lois. "Lamech's Opposite." *En-Gedi Resource Center*, July 3, 2015. https://engediresourcecenter.com/2015/07/03/lamechs-opposite/.

Universal Co-Masonry. "King Solomon's Temple." https://www.universalfreemasonry.org/en/history-freemasonry/king-solomon-temple.

Vail, Kenneth. "Clay Routledge: The Religious Mind is in the Heart." *Psychology Today*, July 2, 2018. https://www.psychologytoday.com/us/blog/tree-life/201807/clay-routledge-the-religious-mind-is-in-the-heart.

Vallée, Jacques. *Dimensions: A Casebook of Alien Contact.*

Charlottesville: Anomalist Books, 2008.

———. The Invisible College: What a Group of Scientists Has Discovered About UFO Influence on the Human Race. *Charlottesville: Anomalist Books, 2014.*

Vance, Ashlee. "Merely Human? That's So Yesterday." *New York Times,* June 12, 2010. https://www.nytimes.com/2010/06/13/business/13sing.html.

Van den Broek, Roel. *The Myth of the Phoenix, According to Classical and Early Christian Traditions.* Leiden: E.J. Brill. 1972.

Wade, Lizzie. "Ancient DNA reveals fate of the mysterious Canaanites." *Science,* July 27, 2017. https://www.sciencemag.org/news/2017/07/ancient-dna-reveals-fate-mysterious-canaanites.

Wasson, Donald L. "Gades" *Ancient History Encyclopedia*, March 8, 2013. https://www.ancient.eu/Gades/.

Watch Tower Bible and Tract Society. "Genealogy of Jesus Christ." In vol. 1 of *Insight on the Scriptures.* New York: Watchtower Bible and Tract Society, 1988.

Williams, Henry Smith. "The Phoenician Time of Power." In Vol. 2 *of The Historians' History of the World.* New York: Encyclopedia Britannica, 1902. https://www.gutenberg.org/files/52177/52177-h/52177-h.htm.

Made in the USA
Las Vegas, NV
07 March 2022

45179510R00111